THE ART OF
COMPASSION

THE ART OF COMPASSION

STORIES OF MUSIC AND JUSTICE FROM
Michael W. Smith, Martin and Anna Smith,
Darlene Zschech, Chris Tomlin, Matt Redman,
Tim Hughes, Steven Curtis Chapman,
Paul Baloche, Andy Park, Graham Kendrick,
Stu Garrard, Israel Houghton

Edited by Craig Borlase

New York   Boston   Nashville

Edited by Craig Borlase.
All photos are copyright of Martin Smith, Andy Hutch, and Dave Dobson.
Cover art direction Mark Debnam.
*Adm. by Kingswaysongs.com for Europe (excluding Germany, Austria, Switzerland, Liechtenstein, and Luxembourg). tym@kingsway.co.uk. Used by permission.

FaithWords
Hachette Book Group
237 Park Avenue
New York, NY 10017

Visit our Web site at www.faithwords.com.

Printed in the United States of America

First Edition: January 2009
10 9 8 7 6 5 4 3 2 1

FaithWords is a division of Hachette Book Group, Inc.
The FaithWords name and logo are trademarks of Hachette Book Group, Inc.

LCCN: 2008940824
ISBN: 978-0-446-54687-4

TO FARIN, WITH ALL OUR LOVE.
IT WAS YOUR SMILE THAT BROKE OUR HEARTS.
WE HOPE THIS BOOK WILL BE THE VOICE YOU DON'T HAVE.

CONTENTS

ACKNOWLEDGMENTS   ix
INTRODUCTION / CRAIG BORLASE   xi

THE STORY OF COMPASSIONART / MICHAEL W. SMITH   1
THE COMPASSIONART DIARIES / MARTIN AND ANNA SMITH   15
RISE UP, CHURCH! / DARLENE ZSCHECH   39
TOWELS AND SOCKS / CHRIS TOMLIN   53
JOURNEYS WITHOUT A PASSPORT / MATT REDMAN   69
THE MIDDLE OF THE ROOM / TIM HUGHES   87
A VISIBLE GOSPEL / STEVEN CURTIS CHAPMAN   109
BAREFOOT ON THE MOUNTAIN / PAUL BALOCHE   125
FRIENDS OF THE POOR / ANDY PARK   137
LOOKING TO THE FUTURE / GRAHAM AND TAMSIN KENDRICK   159
MY ALLERGIC REACTION / STU GARRARD   183
FIVE QUESTIONS I WANT TO ASK / ISRAEL HOUGHTON   201

EPILOGUE / BISHOP GRAHAM CRAY   215
THE STORY OF COMPASSIONART   227

ACKNOWLEDGMENTS

Someone once told me that it's not more money we need but just great ideas. Time will tell if CompassionArt is one of those 'ideas' or just a music project that came and went. One thing I do know, though, is that my friends and I became a team, twelve individuals used to scoring great goals on their own working together as match-winners. The songs are better for it, the friendship sweeter for it and the future much brighter for it.

I would like to acknowledge the many people who helped Anna and me pull this CompassionArt team together.

First my brother Paul and his wife Pip, who supported us from the very start. You have sacrificed much to help get this dream out of the ground: thank you.

To Brett Farrell for all your legal help: we would have been in serious trouble without you! To Bill Hearn at EMI for driving through the structure and cutting through the red tape for this vision to happen. To the CompassionArt trustees, Richard Hubbard, Mark Zschech, Dave Meyer, Brett Farrell, Bill Hearn and Matt Redman. This is going to be a crazy ride!

To my pastor David Thatcher and all at Arun Community Church for the years of doing life together. To Joyce and Dave Meyer for taking us around the world. Thanks for kick-starting the rest of our lives and giving us something new to sing about. To Graham Cray for keeping these songs on the straight and narrow!

To my bandmates in Delirious?, Tim, Paul, Stu G and Jon. Thanks for giving me the space to grow into this. To Tony Patoto for managing the American office. To Jonathan Brown, Stew Smith, Mark Debnam, Clive Sherwood and all at Fierce! Distribution. To Les Moir for producing the record with me: thank you for your energy in turning the dream into a product. I will never forget our time in the studio.

To the film crew in Scotland: Andy Hutch, Tim and Mairi Neeves, and Ian Hamilton at Compassion UK for letting us use your cameras. To Dave Dobson for photographs. To Missy Cattle for the title of the book. To Jon Thatcher, Steve Winton and Contrapositive for getting the website off the ground. To Christian Andre for the coffee, Craig A. Anderson for the painting and Jedidiah for the T-shirts. To Tamsin Kendrick for the initial artist interviews at Abbey Road. To Jim McNeish and team for letting us take over your house in Scotland to write these songs.

A big thank you to Katherine Venn, our book editor and all at Hodder & Stoughton and FaithWords. Can you believe we got this book together in two months!

To my friends the songwriters, Michael, Chris, Darlene, Andy, Stu G, Tim, Matt, Graham, Israel, Steven and Paul. We did it, we broke the mold and gave ourselves to something greater. The songs we wrote could actually rescue people from poverty; thanks for turning up and giving birth to this. I will never ever forget our time in Scotland.

Of course, huge thanks to Craig Borlase for taking these interviews and turning them into twelve chapters that read well: you have done a brilliant job in an extraordinarily painful time. We dedicate this book to your Moses-ladies, who passed away during the writing of this book.

Last but not least, my wife Anna. I still remember our first conversation about gathering all our writer friends together. Through all of this I have been humbled by your passion for justice and your extraordinary grace. I love you.

To my children, Elle-Anna, Noah, Indi-Anna, Levi, Ruby-Anna and Mary-Anna: you have carried this with your mum and dad too; let justice run through your veins all the days of your life.

Martin Smith
May 2008

INTRODUCTION

Craig Borlase

I REMEMBER THE FIRST TIME I HEARD ABOUT COMPASSIONART. MY WIFE AND I WERE EATING WITH FRIENDS — FRIENDS WHO HAD HEARD AT FIRST HAND MARTIN'S HALF-FORMED PLANS THE SUMMER BEFORE THINGS ALL KICKED OFF. I DON'T REMEMBER WHAT WE WERE EATING, BUT I REMEMBER WHAT I THOUGHT ABOUT IT ALL.

I didn't think much of the idea.

What possible good could come of a bunch of wealthy Christians flying from across the oceans to slap each other's backs and fiddle with their guitars? It was . . . well, I don't know what I thought it was. I just knew I wasn't all that excited.

I don't know what happened, but somewhere across the nine months that passed between then and now I changed my mind and my heart. Slowly at first, then with gathering pace, I began to see what this CompassionArt project could achieve. I saw the sacrifice made by each member, the openness and honesty, the passion for being a part of something that was aiming at nothing lower than changing the world. I realized that it was me that was stupid and self-indulgent.

★

Let me give you a little background. CompassionArt started when Martin and Anna Smith wondered what might happen if Christian songwriters got together, wrote songs and gave away every penny that they generated. What started as a slightly crazy idea rapidly became a set of concrete plans. Before long, CompassionArt found life: with twelve musicians retreating for a week in January 2008 to write, then coming back in February to record an album that tried to join the dots between faith, worship and the horrific level of injustice that surrounds us.

At some point someone talked about a book. What started out as the kind of book with nice pictures and few words eventually became this: a wad of pages across which the twelve people who had attended the retreat tried to find a whole load more words to explain what they thought about compassion.

Books like this are not supposed to come together in this way. They're supposed to take time – the kind of time that makes the passing of the seasons look like morning rush hour. They're supposed to require complex skills of negotiation as writers and editors work out how much trust exists between them. They're supposed to be complex, complicated and – at the end of the day – probably not all that good. After all, isn't this just another bit of branding, another "product" put out to make some cash on the back of the other, more high-profile releases in the CompassionArt "series"? No one really expects a book like this to change their life. Do they?

But none of the above is true when it comes to discussing these pages you're holding in your hands. None of the above sums up the process, the path and the outcome. None of it is right.

The Art of Compassion took just a couple of months to write. None of the names on the front jockeyed for position or held tight to their message or polished their ego. And – for me – the job of playing midwife as these words have come to life has changed my own. Neither I nor my family will ever be the same again. CompassionArt has changed us forever.

I buried my mother while working on this book. Her nineteen-month battle with cancer ended the day after I agreed to take it on. In the days that followed – days stained with despair and an aching sense of loss and sadness – I was only able to think about CompassionArt for a few seconds at a time. Could I still be involved? Was it wise – would I lose my grief if I stuck my head into a book so soon? Could I even find the words any more? Did any of it actually matter at all? Was it worth it?

It turns out that all those questions were easily answered.

I hope that these words help. Across these pages you'll find stories of suffering, chaos and pain. You'll find hope, help and genuine, faith-soaked optimism too. You'll read words that come from the mouths of those who usually give us melodies and harmonies and songs that bring us closer to God. But these words you'll read now will be different – there's pain among them, confusion and frustration. There's pride in the sacrifice of others and gratitude that God has allowed them to join in.

None of them are experts about any of this, and that is where this book is unlike all those others that tackle the subjects of poverty and faith. These twelve people are not professional theologians, aid workers, campaigners or development specialists. They're people who – like the rest of us – wonder how their lives can be more effective when it comes to fighting poverty and getting closer to God's agenda for us all.

★

God's agenda . . . I hope some of you will already have your minds made up about it. I hope this serves as more fuel for your fire, a whole bucket of flammables that leaves you pushed further out to put faith into action.

And I hope others will be doubtful about it all. I hope you start this book with a cynicism about it all. If you give it time and space and allow these words the concentration and debate they need, I hope you'll come out the other side a little more convinced of our collective ability and responsibility to offer whole-life hope to the world that is so scarred by need.

"The local church is the hope of the world." You'll probably read that phrase way too many times across these chapters. I'm sorry for the repetition. No, actually, I'm not. It's a phrase that needs to be pressed into us. It's a phrase that articulates our responsibility to be agents of human justice in the world. And it's a phrase that's utterly soaked in optimism and excitement.

There are temptations all around us. The chances are that it won't take you too long to remember some of the ones that have drifted through your mind over the last twenty-four hours. But while some of them are obvious, there's a range of temptations that are subtle and sometimes harder to spot.

Take this one, for example: our lives don't matter that much.

This myth comes in many forms, plaguing us with thoughts about it being God's business and not ours, that we are too small or that the world's problems are just too great.

But if we choose to give in to these temptations we'll be left muzzled, blindfolded and deaf, like those three "wise" monkeys all wrapped up in one. Giving up on action cuts into our potential and reduces our impact. Giving up on our potential to change the world around us is giving up on God.

There's more to being alive today than being a monkey, no matter how wise.

In the days of the early Church, with its ever-increasing roll call of martyrs, the numbers of Jews and non-Jews joining the Christian sect grew with phenomenal power. By the end of the first century – and not more than seventy years after Christ's handful of followers were told to go and make disciples – there are as many as one million Christians spread across the Roman empire. Within another three centuries, forty million people would count themselves as Christians – almost a quarter of the world's population.

The numbers are different today. There are even more of us: almost one in three of the world's six billion people are Christians. Within the next week we could do more to change the state of the world than any single government could do in a decade. We are, quite clearly, the hope of the world – and what a truly awesome hope that is.

♥

Biblical themes don't come much stronger than this: God's offer of relationship with his created beings and our flip-flopping between responsibility and apathy, between being the bringers of the blessing and being trapped by the bubble.

It was just this way with the Israelites while they were held captive by the injustice of Pharaoh's reign. They found themselves at the wrong end of a power system designed to protect the interests of those at the top. Fortunately for us, God's plans were bigger than the Egyptian restrictions:

The LORD said, "I have indeed seen the misery of my people in Egypt. I have heard them crying out because of their slave drivers, and I am

Craig Borlase **xvii**

concerned about their suffering. So I have come down to rescue them from the hand of the Egyptians and to bring them up out of that land into a good and spacious land, a land flowing with milk and honey . . . And now the cry of the Israelites has reached me, and I have seen the way the Egyptians are oppressing them. So now, go. I am sending you to Pharaoh to bring my people the Israelites out of Egypt."

Exodus 3:7-10

Look again at God's speech. It makes such a great start, like an Oscar-winning warm-up to one of those explosive sequences where the good guy ends up in his vest, trashing the town and trouncing the baddies. The fact that God declares that he has "seen the misery . . . heard [the] crying" and has "come down to rescue them" would surely have got Moses settling back into his armchair and rubbing his hands in eager anticipation at the remarkable spectacle about to be witnessed. Then comes something unexpected: "I am sending *you*," the killer line, the counterpoint that shifts the tone as God places Moses at the heart of his plan.

"You," God says: singular, not plural. "You," alone, impetuous, unwise and wholly unqualified to do the job. "You," overwhelmed and dwarfed by the task. "You," worrying about how on earth you're going to make a difference.

We all know what followed. We know that God's power to save was more than enough without the input of Moses, but that through his grace Moses was invited into partnership with God, to be the waiter who delivered the order. Does God want us as ready-made heroes? I doubt it. Surely he'd rather we were on our knees, aware of all the reasons why we can't match up, but ready to obey all the same.

As I add these final words — barely three months after starting to work on this book – death and funerals are once more a part of my house. My mother-in-law died tonight. Her battle, like my mother's, was with cancer. Both my and my wife's mother shared a type of faith that propelled them out to engage with the world beyond the Church – a world scarred by alienation, isolation and poverty. They were – and still are – the Moses-ladies I look up to, the ones I know for sure would have understood far more than I what it means to talk about – and then get on and put into action – the art of compassion.

Craig Borlase
May 2008

THE STORY OF COMPASSIONART

Michael W. Smith

YOU WANT TO KNOW HOW YOU COME TO BE HOLDING THIS BOOK IN YOUR HANDS? IF YOU LIKE I CAN TELL YOU PART OF THE STORY — THE ONE OF HOW THESE PAGES CAME TO BE MADE, OF HOW THE WORDS FELL INTO PLACE AND THE SONGS TOOK SHAPE ABOVE THEM. I CAN TELL YOU ABOUT THE BIRTH OF COMPASSIONART, OF THE IDEAS AND THE HOPES AND THE WAY THAT PIECE BY PIECE IT HAS COME TOGETHER SO FAR. I'LL TELL YOU ABOUT THE POVERTY AND THE SENSE OF PURPOSE AND THE HOPE THAT TOGETHER WE MIGHT BE ABLE TO DO SOMETHING BETTER THAN WE CAN ON OUR OWN.

I'm hoping that by the time we get to the end of our story so far you'll see that there's a greater story within all of this: a story that's yet to be written: a story all about what you did next.

★

It was in 2006 that I got a call from Martin Smith. I'd known him first as the front man of Delirious?, then as a guy who has become a dear friend and writing partner. Anyway, he told me he had a wild idea. I like wild ideas. He was talking away at me, saying, "Wouldn't it be great if we pulled together a whole load of artists and writers and tucked ourselves away in some castle in Europe? And what if we wrote songs? And what if they helped to inspire the Church in new ways to engage with the world? And what if we were to make absolutely no money out of it at all? And what if we figured out a way to donate all those proceeds to the poorest of the poor?"

And that's CompassionArt. A bunch of people make something, give up any claim to earning any money out of it and then plough their royalties back into improving the lives of those gripped by poverty around the world. It's as simple as it is wild.

Martin didn't actually get this far in his explanation to me before I was in. My heart was signed up from the moment he finished his first sentence.

But how do we pull it off?

Scheduling. That was the big thing, the largest potential barrier to it all. The least of our worries was that it would resonate with people's hearts. We know a lot of people who really want to change the world, and I'm one of them. But scheduling? That's a whole other problem. Everyone has a busy life; everyone has their own things going on. So how do we carve out a piece of time when all these people can follow Martin to some crazy European castle?

It had to be January. Since Christmas and New Year were out of the way and most people were on holiday, it was our best opportunity. So back in 2006 I, and many others, marked off our calendars for the second week of 2008.

Then all the work started. The planning, the details, the logistics . . .

Before I knew it I found myself in a big old house beside a loch in Scotland. It was no castle, but it was better – a place soaked in a sense that something significant was about to happen.

And it did. It was a week that for the rest of my life I will never forget.

♥

On the first day Martin put us into groups and told us who was going to hibernate with who in what room. Then two hours later we were to meet back together as a group with a song.

That's not the way I work. When I've tried to do that in the past it's been a bit of a disaster. We're all a little anxious because when you're thrown into a room with two or three other people you probably haven't written with before . . . let's just say that it takes a little getting used to.

That first session presented a tough choice: we each had to decide if we were going to be the one to throw out the first idea. Were we ready to make ourselves raw — to expose what we had and put an idea out for the other two or three to taste?

Once we made it through that first session we moved on to dissecting the songs as a whole group. If writing in a small group didn't feel vulnerable enough, we then had eleven others critique our work as we sat silently and looked on. The rule was made that we couldn't talk if we had been involved with the song being discussed.

Even though that process felt raw, it immediately became clear that we were there for a greater cause: that there was something bigger going on other than a few guys playing chords and throwing around lyrics.

How come? It was a little bit of a glimpse of the body of Christ as it worked on a wonderful and beautiful level that I had never experienced. Throughout the week it kept on getting better and better and better; we were all unified — we had nothing to lose. As every song we wrote was thrown into the CompassionArt pot, we began to build up a foundation. We all wrote the songs — nobody could really remember who'd had a hand in what. Many of us had never been in a place like this before.

And that's why it changed my life.

★

Without question, the vulnerability and intimacy of the whole thing was important, but it would have been nothing without the focus. Each of us held in mind images and memories of encounters with the very people we were hoping that these songs would help. I went back in my mind to times when I was holding babies that I knew died two weeks later; I remembered Kibera – one of the largest slums in Africa – which I had visited the year before. I thought of being outside Cape Town in a shanty town of half a million people where one in four have the HIV virus. I then remembered being in a hospital where the HIV medications were working – where the miraculous was being absorbed and lives were being saved for just a few dollars. This is what I thought about as I sang.

Of course, I've not shared their experience of poverty, because I was born into middle-class America. I've been blessed to have never known what it's like to go without food for a day, other than the times I've been led to fast. But when I held a baby whose final days were drawing near, whose remaining life could be counted in hours rather than weeks, months or years – those feelings never really leave you.

All around the house we had pictures up on the walls – images of those we were trying to help. We would catch just a glimpse of them throughout the day and it would take us right back to those experiences. Compassion had a face and our time there had a purpose.

In one session Darlene, Israel and I were in a room together. I think Martin came in on the latter part of it, but I can't really remember what went down. Perhaps it was Israel who had some sort of melody idea for the verse and then I just jumped on the piano and sort of went off to the races. And all of a sudden we were singing:

For he is good, for he is faithful ... so great, so great, and your love endures for ever to the end of the age.

Lyrically we were hashing it out, but the heart of it was there in an instant.

And that's the way things went. People would come back from their two-hour huddles with songs and lyrics and ideas, and a sense that together we were finding words and melodies and themes that were bigger than anything we could have hoped for. At the end of the week we had more songs than we ever planned: twenty-two in all.

Five weeks later we were in the Abbey Road studios, London. The walls are dripping with atmosphere and a sense of significance ... even the Beatles had been there. But there was more to it all than that. Once again we sensed that these songs were bigger than anything we could have built – they were being driven by a far more powerful force.

Three days later we had fifteen songs recorded.

It doesn't usually happen that way. Time just never seems to allow so much to be achieved in so few hours.

And then we wrote this book! Technically there was too little time for a book, but we had too much momentum and too many messages and stories to tell to let the deadlines stop us.

CompassionArt has been a life-changing experience for me on such a personal level. I worked with so many people and we accomplished so much. We came back with so many songs when our goal had been to write just one each. That couldn't have happened if everyone hadn't decided to drop their egos at the door. I came away convinced and challenged to find a way to make my CompassionArt experience happen in my everyday life: to be open and unified with others instead of giving in to the temptation to have your guard up all the time.

There were times when the Bishop was leading us in communion and devotions, where the unity and the creativity that left us smiling as we went to sleep at night was still there in abundance the next morning! Everything about it left us all mopping up the tears after a meltdown every day. There was something going on that was inexplicable. All I can tell you is that it was the Holy Spirit. When you have those kinds of encounters it changes you. I believe that when we come to a place where we realize that it's really *really* not about us, our perspective changes to where we can see that it's the eternal things that really matter. When this happens I believe that we're able to tap into the well of creativity on a more consistent basis.

♥

WHAT COULD ALL THIS MEAN?

Nothing about this is limited to the twelve people who went to that big old house by the loch in Scotland. Nothing at all says that this stops there. Nothing says the story ends with an album, a book and a website.

Could this be a model for other artists from other genres to use? What would it be like if the rock stars or the country stars, the hip hop stars or the alternatives did something similar? How many millions could be raised and given away? Does poverty have a voice that says, "There's only so much that we need"? No way. The truth is that the poorest of the poor need billions upon billions to lift them free from poverty.

But is this limited to artists with record deals? How can it be? Surely you could do this with a business – even a small business like the chicken take-out place on the corner, the print shops around the shopping center or even the coffee shops in the neighborhood. Just take the model and run with it. Get together and give away your time and talent for free to produce something that you can sell, and then donate all the money to help fight poverty. It's really that simple and plenty of people can truly play a part in it. So I hope this inspires you – that somewhere, right now, inside you there's a part that gets excited when you think about what all of this could lead to down the road.

And I think you might.

If we take a look around us we'll see a generation that is passionate about changing the world. The fact that college students, school students and people of all ages are taking time out of their lives to leave their comfort zones and help those from the other ends of the world who are affected by the AIDS crisis or the war in Iraq, instead of just soaking up the good times for themselves, underlines the fact that the welfare of others is on the front burner of people's minds far more these days than it was fifteen or twenty years ago. Isn't it clear that there are a lot of people who see things this way – we want to see the West stand up for the poor?

When we look out beyond the boundaries of our own lives – whether we start to focus on the people living around us, on the needs of our country or on the problems that trouble people throughout the world – we uncover one of the greatest secrets of eternity: that giving away is better than holding on, that connecting with others for their benefit far outweighs a life of greedy isolation.

SOMEONE ELSE'S STORY

If I hadn't worked this out already, the last few years have given me hundreds of real-time experiences to drive the message home. I've had the privilege of serving as co-chairman of the President's Council on Civic Participation and Volunteerism. It's a grand name, and it's an impressive body. After all, when your group exists because the President of the United States expressly wishes it, you know you've got momentum.

Our purpose is simple, but profound: we honor those who are making a difference in the world. We want to give people a small reward for their efforts and hopefully inspire others to take up their own causes and change their own worlds. The whole concept comes from the idea that governments can't change people's hearts – only people can.

During the couple of times a year we get together as a council I often feel unqualified. I'm a singer, wearing a suit, and I have to sit down for eight hours – it feels a little unfamiliar, but it's an inspirational experience to say the least.

We see corporations donating two hours a week of their employees' time to mentoring young kids in inner cities – hours that add up to be worth millions and millions of dollars. We get to meet the individuals face to face who are doing a lot of this remarkable work.

Being on tour means that I get to meet some of these unsung heroes who really are changing our world. From time to time I'll stop a show to honor them with the President's Volunteer Service Award. I remember the little old lady who has set up a handful of orphanages in Africa and the nondescript guy who just happens to have donated more time than you could possibly imagine to helping the local homeless. Neither of them probably even want the award or the publicity as they, like so many others, know that their reward is eternal. But average, ordinary, plain-looking people like these are heroes to the thousands who stand up to applaud them.

As they come up on stage I'm bursting at the seams because, other than my own children, little makes me happier than to see someone do something for someone else. When you see someone who really is making a difference in the world it's hard not to get emotional; especially as I watch the audience and you see them begin to cry and get caught up in it all. Right then you know, you just know, that this is a pivotal night. You know that many of those people are going to go home and re-evaluate their lives because of the little old lady or this ordinary guy that they've just seen climb up on stage. And it's not because they want the award, it's because they're alive to the fact that when we give to others – when we live our lives in a way that improves the world around us – it's then that we find ourselves living life to the fullest.

I'm going to tell one final story. It starts in August, 1988. There's a lady called Glenda Gleaves who lives in Florida working as an air traffic controller. One day when she's on a break from controlling the skies she finds that she's doodled, scribbled and drawn all over a flight plan. She looks down to find that this is no longer a plan for a flight, but an outline for a way to help support families that are under pressure.

Glenda thinks that God must have a pretty good sense of humor since her first marriage had ended so horribly. But the vision has been planted and there is no doubting the power it already holds.

She has a name for it – Family Affair Ministries – as well as a sense that this God-given vision has more than a single facet. It must not settle for simply offering nice words and useful handouts to those in need: it must aim as high as it possibly can, to restore families and rebuild communities – all through God's hand extended. As she reads those last words back to herself, she realizes that she's already got a mission statement.

Glenda goes to her pastor to get his take on it all. He likes the idea and gives her his blessing, but tells her she needs to prepare for a journey that will change her life for ever. He gives her three bottles of oil and says goodbye.

Back home, Glenda talks it through with her sons. They get impacted by Luke 14:28:

Suppose one of you wants to build a tower. Will he not first sit down and estimate the cost to see if he has enough money to complete it?

In response to this verse they give away their possessions. Why? Because she knows that they must give up all that represents natural stability and comfort if they are to see God's power in its full effect. She knows that she must obey God no matter what.

A little while later and Glenda and her sons are on a Greyhound bus heading to Nashville, Tennessee.

Once in Nashville they spend twenty-one days living in a mission, giving Glenda the opportunity to truly know what homelessness feels like. In her past she has been battered, so she understands abuse, and since moving she knows what it is to rely on others for charity to ensure survival, allowing her to understand what it's like to rebuild your life from nothing.

Glenda and her sons are given a home in the largest public housing project in Nashville. Their new neighborhood offers an overwhelming range of need: young, single mothers trying to hold life together, grandmothers raising their grandchildren, a community scarred by poverty and neglect.

Glenda teaches the young mothers how to budget, plan meals and shop for groceries. She also mentors them in parenting and helps their children with schoolwork. Her sons, Dale and Sean, alongside their mother, begin one-to-one reading sessions with the children. They begin to understood first-hand the challenges that their neighbors feel. In time they will stand up as advocates for more and more of them, and soon the stories of hope will be told by those whose lives have been transformed by the simple acts of a devoted woman of God.

The work has not been without cost for Glenda and her family, but their giving goes beyond all those ideas of counting up the hours. They know – like many, many other remarkable Christians around the world – that life is lived better when it is lived with others in mind.

♥

So here we are, at the end of the introductions. It's time for others to tell their stories now. Keep reading and you'll hear about how the other writers have watched as their hearts have been pulled and stretched by contact with a world beyond stages and airports. You'll read about the hopes that people have, the ambitions that we can strive for and the possibilities that lie within our very own hands.

I hope you'll learn to appreciate the art of compassion. I hope it makes sense. I hope you see its beauty and its power, and I hope it leaves you desperate to get out and see what your own hands can make when compassion captures your heart.

THE
COMPASSIONART
DIARIES

Martin and
Anna Smith

★ **14 JANUARY 2006; HYDERABAD, INDIA**

Playing some concerts out here, working with a preacher by the name of Joyce Meyer.

There were 400,000 in the crowd tonight. Never seen anything like it.

Still churning over the day, went to visit a feeding project in a rural village, it blew my mind.

I worry if my cappuccino is the right temperature, these people were lucky to find clean drinking water. It bothers me, what have I become? I'm wrestling. I call home, Anna full on getting dinner for five kids, how can I explain what is happening to me?

♥ **14 JANUARY 2006; LITTLEHAMPTON, ENGLAND**

Mart phoned, there was something different in his voice, I don't know how to process this to be honest, he seems troubled by what he's seen. I'm left here holding the fort and he's getting all "emotional" about someone else's kids. I need him here, our children miss their dad.

★ **27 JUNE 2006**

I love writing songs with other people, it's a great honor. Last month with Michael W. was good – the words just seemed to come and the melodies offered themselves up. Reminds me of that Keith

Richards quote about how the greatest melodies are already written, how all we have to do is work out how to pluck them out of the air. The fun is that we're still all looking for them!

★ 2 JULY 2006

It was one of those wall-planner days again where we tried to take another look at next year. It's always tense – trying to find the balance between the gigs that will pay for the wages throughout the office, the ones that we have a hunch about and the others that we need to do to keep the momentum up. And then there's the whole plot of how much time we spend away anyway. Our "not away for more than ten days" rule has been broken a few times already, and because of the new "industry climate" we are struggling to stick to it much longer. It used to be just here and America. Not anymore. We knew that calling the album *World Service* was right, but we never guessed how accurate it would be.

★ 13 JULY 2006

Another writing day with another mate. This time with Matt. I remember when he first came to the studio I worked at down on the Littlehampton marina. Matt showed up with a guitar he couldn't tune and a plastic carrier bag that spewed sheets of paper with lyrics and chord sheets. It wasn't so much that he was nervous, it was more that he just desperately wanted to get it right. And he did.

Anyway, he's changed a lot since then. We all have. We've grown up, got homes with space and passports with too many creases. We wrote for most of the afternoon kicking around ideas. Then we laughed as my kids danced around the living room.

Just as he left we talked about doing it again. No plans as yet, but it would be good to get it in the diary.

♥ **15 JULY 2006**

There are all these amazing people wanting to work with us, and I think I feel a bit surprised. I don't think I ever really guessed that they would – you know, 'cause these are some big names, they're people I've looked up to for ages. And I feel excited about it all too, it feels like something else is stirring, like something might be building.

★ **10 AUGUST 2006**

The kids have finished school, we're off the road and off on holiday. A short flight to Europe with too much luggage and the hope of sunshine.

Had a thought a minute ago that I wanted to get down before we leave at 6 a.m. tomorrow: wouldn't it be great to get a whole load of people together – other writers – and come up with some great songs for the Church? All those times of late, writing with Michael and Matt, Darlene, Graham and Tim have got me thinking: how good could it be if we all spent a week together coming up with a new wave of anthems and soundtracks?

★ **11 AUGUST 2006**

Just about to leave – not long enough to write more than this: woke up remembering India, there's no point in doing that songwriting idea with everyone if we're going make money out of it. That would be stupid. Have to give it away.

♥ 21 AUGUST 2006

A few weeks back, before we came out here on holiday, we were lying in bed talking about the way that he's been working with all these people. He's right; we ought to get them all together for a week to write. It sounds amazing, maybe historic. No idea how we're gonna fit this in!

★ 7 SEPTEMBER 2006

Called Matt and brought up the idea of a songwriters' retreat that gives all the royalties away. I had a whole speech ready: how the decision to give it all away was central to the whole thing, how we've all been blessed and gained loads from the Christian music industry, but now it's time to put something back. If that's what we mean by modeling something, then so be it.

Anyway, this speech I'd prepared wasn't needed. I got thirty seconds into telling him about it and he was jumping all over it, saying how great he thought it was.

Same with Darlene and Mark.

Looks like this could be something with more life in it than I first thought. Could this be something that makes God smile?

★ 20 OCTOBER 2006

My first big phone call with Bill Hearn, CEO of EMI Christian Music Group in Nashville.

I've been friends with Bill for years, I was expecting him to be mad with me for trying to buck the system; I was asking a lot, for EMI publishing to release their artists from their deals to be a part of this project.

"Yes, let's do it," he said. I didn't have to fight, there were no boxing gloves, he fell in love with the idea and opened the doors wide for me to talk to all the key people.

★ **18 DECEMBER 2006**

Officially invited all twelve writers today for January 2008.

I get around to talking to the other music publishers involved; a mixture of responses, I don't have the same relationships with all of them but all good people, great people wanting to use their influence. Everyone knows deep down that this is a chance to change a piece of the world.

Loads more phone calls, red tape. I'm a singer not a politician, but hey, it's a new day.

♥ **18 DECEMBER 2006**

People's eyes light up when Mart says about it all. I remember last April being in a hotel room in Nashville with Michael, Darlene and Mark, Chris Tomlin and us – and there was a connection. Mart was talking about it then, there was something in the room that was amazing: the sense that we could do something together bigger than who we are. We just knew that this journey began that night.

Also been thinking about the fact that this could bring money in. And we could do something else with it. But I don't have a clue what.

We can know so much about the world – through the television, through the Church – there are so many things that we could do, but it's overwhelming to know what to do. I'd like it to be something I was passionate about though.

I'm not a charity worker, I'm a mum – I don't have the answers. But we have to do our bit.

★ 5 JANUARY 2007

Great. Things are a little different now. Smitty's on board. So's Tim and Tomlin, as well as Matt and Darlene. When I spoke with the last lot of publishers this afternoon something had changed. There are too many of us on board now – too many of those big names that the whole thing finally has enough momentum to push this all the way. I guess that's what happens when the idea's clean and nobody makes a plan to benefit from it financially.

Realized we can't do this on our own, I ask my brother Paul to work on CompassionArt for one day a week, a new day for him. Talked to a music lawyer today, Brett Farrell, he says he's in and will help, can't believe the favor on this.

★ 9 JANUARY 2007

We just arrived in Mumbai, India. We're here on tour, and last night we played a gig in Hyderabad. It was surreal: 10,000 people in a field; PA strung up with tape and homemade power points; crazy-fast drivers to and from the airport and a sense that something bigger is in the air.

Stu G's all messed up.

His heart's caved in by the poverty, beaten by the fact that even our suitcases cost more than a year's wages for some of these people – let alone the stuff inside them.

He says he's feeling uncomfortable – but it's not about here, it's about our comfortable lives back home.

Anyway, Mumbai's like nothing else. We've seen poverty before – we've been around Mexico and parts of Colombia – but Mumbai is something else.

Everyone's working. I didn't think that would bother me, but the fact that everyone – of every age – is out, whether sweeping the road with improvised brooms made out of branches and twigs or selling whatever they've found or made or done whatever to get. Even the people that crowd the windows as we wait for the lights to change, even they're working, so I'm told. Most of these guys that are begging – mainly girls and young women with half-asleep babies – are being pimped to be there. And those half-asleep babies aren't their own. They're borrowed, rented or taken. And they're not naturally sleepy; some of them are drugged to make them more docile and cute.

Mumbai is something else.

★ 10 JANUARY 2007

The trip there was intense. The bus struggled as we pulled into the sidestreet and parked opposite a hundred different stalls and workshops and shacks and homes. The noise was beyond white noise – it was all different colors, a thousand saris all at the same time.

We were here to see Prem Kiran. It's a project that works with children of prostitutes, as well as their families. I never had any idea quite how much was going to have happened in me by the time I got back on the bus.

Seventy children in a single room. Happy faces. All singing. One girl can't stop looking at me and I can't stop looking at her. This girl – Farin (you pronounce it *fa-reen*) – she's a beautiful-looking girl, and I know that something is happening inside me. What it is, I don't know. But I know it's big. There's something about the life that's within her, the sense that her beauty and grace shine out above and beyond this place with its crumbling streets and open sewers.

Prem Kiran has fed, clothed, sheltered and educated Farin for a while. She's obviously bright and the place is good to her. She's happy there, so why does my heart beat like this? Why do I feel as if this random eleven-year-old girl in a city of twenty-four million has just pulled my guts out? Why do I feel as though every fiber of my soul is exposed?

Our guide – Pastor Umale – tells me that Farin's mother is a prostitute. A working prostitute. My mind and heart beat even faster.

He asks us if we'd like to go and see what kind of places these families live in.

I am nervous, but I say yes. I couldn't tell you about the others – I guess Stu G was still messed up and Jon, Stew and Tim were feeling the same, but I don't know for sure.

We tread the path to the houses. They're not houses, though, they're a few bricks, a collection of pens with roofs and doors and not much else. They have taps that offer clean water at a trickle, but these homes are like nothing I've ever seen before. I'm close to being sick as we walk around, treading over the sewer and feeling so dumb for wearing flip-flops. It's the spirit of the place as well as the smell that's getting me – the fact that under these beds children hide while their mothers collect a few rupees from men they have sex with.

How many times has Farin lain under the bed while her mother has worked? How many cries has she had to stifle, how many nightmares has she woken up to in her own home? Or has she left the room and wandered the streets? How much more has she seen than my Elle – my own ten-year-old? They could be sisters. But Elle talks about becoming a dancer. What choice does Farin have? How long will it be before she becomes a prostitute?

We get back from our walk, back into the project. Farin is still looking at me. We have to leave. I get in the bus to go back to the hotel and inside I'm dying. I've never felt this feeling before. I want to take her home, to protect her. I don't know what or why or how it's happened, but I know what I feel: that I am her father.

★ 11 JANUARY 2007

I couldn't get Farin off my mind for the rest of the day. Today it's been no different. I wake up and I see her. I can't get her off my mind. I'm wondering: is it possible to bring her to England and (I can't believe I'm even going to write this word) adopt her? Is it just madness to take someone out of their culture? I haven't even been able to talk to Anna about this yet, so how can I be really thinking about adoption? The trip ends tonight – we're in the airport now. These are mad moments – of tears, laughter, soul-searching – all in an airport lounge that's way too crowded and way too bright. I need to get back home.

★ 15 JANUARY 2007

I sat Anna down.

The discussion was big.

I presented the concept: we've got five children already, I've met this little Indian girl who's eleven years old – in itself it's just stupid to even really consider it. But I feel that she belongs in our family. If we don't rescue her then she's going to go into prostitution herself. So why don't we bring her back here to live with us and be a part of our family?

I did it all wrong. Anna and I weren't on the same page. I felt misunderstood, she must have felt let down or over-stretched. It didn't go nearly as well as I hoped. She goes quiet when we talk about it. I wonder what she's thinking.

★ 16 JANUARY 2007

I can't bear it. I'm missing her. I have her photo on my piano. Another's in the studio. I can't get her out of my mind. I've got my own children to think about and look out for. What's going on? Is this what a breakdown looks like? Is that what I'm having here?

♥ 19 JANUARY 2007

Mart had been phoning most evenings while he was in India last week, and he'd been sounding excited, but I'd just assumed that he was caught up in the hype of it all. He's seeing this kind of poverty more now, he's seen a girl and he's all stirred up.

But he came back four days ago and the agency adoption pack is already on the table. The day after he got back we were having Sunday lunch, and he was quite teary. I said, "Are you all right?"

Mart said, "She should be here."

I said, "What do you mean?"

He said, "I'm missing one of my children. She should be with us around the table."

At that moment I lost it inside. You're away loads of the time, I'm pregnant again and looking after our five children, and now you're back and you can't even be here for us. For goodness sake, concentrate on your own children.

But I didn't say anything. This is his journey.

And I didn't feel anything either when he showed me her picture.
But, if God's in this, I'll go with it.

★ 22 JANUARY 2007

Anna's being patient, probably still thinking secretly that I am going mad, but when we talk we're getting further these days. She agrees to talk to a UK adoption agency but gets me to listen as she helps me talk through the enormity of it all. I don't think I've ever faced a decision quite this big in all my life before.

★ 23 JANUARY 2007

The forms are on the side, unopened.

But my heart's still back in India. I've been writing about her – a couple of songs: one about Farin, the other about the gig we did the night we saw Prem Kiran: all the kids and mothers joined us on stage; twelve prostitutes – mothers of the night – dancing to the sounds of heaven.

♥ 2 FEBRUARY 2007

Those adoption papers are still on the side. I'm not going anywhere near them. This all feels very personal – something between him and God – and I've decided what I'm going to do. I'm not going to react or get cross or say too much. I'm not going to be against him, but I've not got the same feelings.

Mart's been on the phone to India all week, trying to work out how he can bring her back. And when I've found that frustrating I've left the room.

And all this is familiar. He gets very passionate about stuff, and I love the fact that he gives his all about things. But that's his character — very captivated, very emotional. And I love him for all that and more.

★ 3 FEBRUARY 2007

The forms are still not filled in, although we've opened them. It costs at least £5,000 to start the process of adopting a child from overseas, and you have to pass some pretty rigorous tests. They come and look at everything about your life — it's an extensive process. But it's not the money or the scrutiny. Or, at least, I don't think it is.

But that's not the point I want to write about. I spoke with Pastor Umale today. It's been something like six weeks since I met Farin. Her mother's changed her mind. She doesn't want to let her go. First she did, but now she doesn't.

What do I feel? I really don't know. Relieved? Yes. Lost? Yes. Hopeless? A little. Angry and determined and desperate? All of the above.

So we make a decision that if we can't adopt her, then let's take care of all seventy kids that live there. Umale told me that the project only costs a few hundred dollars a month to run, so we're going to take care of it. But there's more . . . I know there is.

♥ 3 MARCH 2007

He still talks about Farin a lot. And he's writing songs about her. And I think I'm finding it a little bit hard. He's got his own children, his wife . . . and he's constantly talking about this girl that he's got an affinity with but who's not here.

But it feels like God's in it somehow.

★ 24 MARCH 2007

... and now I can't believe it took me this long to figure it out: of course, this experience with Farin is linked to the songwriting idea. It's all part of the same story, the stuff that happens when God gets hold of your head and heart and floods you with compassion.

And art can make a difference. It doesn't have to be about us – it can drive us out and raise money and teach and inspire and cheer people on as they put faith into action.

So we've got a name and everything now: CompassionArt. I like it. Can't quite tell where it came from, but the fact is that it's all shaping up: we'll get together next January at Jim's place up there in Scotland on the shores of Loch Tay. It's inspiring to just be there – it's the perfect place. And he'll be the ace up the sleeve – with all his insight and wisdom he'll help make the retreat an experience like none of us have ever had before.

★ 2 APRIL 2007

We're going back. It's the least we can do – or, it's the next thing that we have to get around to. This summer – all of us. All the kids, Anna and I and whoever else wants to. We'll visit, see Farin, Umale and the others.

And my heart will break once more – cracked in two by hope and sadness, in equal measure.

♥ 7 MAY 2007

I've been thinking about things. I'm sure that the only way that God could have got Martin to think about poverty and all that was to get his heart. That's why all this happened with Farin: so that God

could get his attention. *By making it feel as though she was his own*
daughter God got his heart. And maybe that's how God is with us.

I don't have that connection with her – maybe I will when I meet
her. But whatever happens, I'm willing to go on the journey,
wherever it ends up.

★ **6 JULY 2007**

It's all busy. Too busy. We just finished some pre-production for the
album, or at least we should have. I spent the last hour torn from
the studio where I was trying to finish some parts and little Indi
had just lost her Nintendo DS game. It was a crisis and everything
had to stop while we all joined in to help Indi find it. And I
suddenly needed to talk with Anna about Farin and how we're
going to keep her from getting trapped by prostitution – it's
bothering me again, and the silence from Umale has got me
thinking that maybe life isn't so set after all. Her future seems to
hang by a thread – a thin strand that if it breaks will leave her
trapped in a life of abuse and disease and horror from which she'll
be all but powerless to escape.

♥ **6 AUGUST 2007**

We've arrived in Hyderabad and tomorrow we leave for Mumbai.
Usual thoughts in my head – about what we need to take and all the
practical things – but some other thoughts too.

I need things to be clear in my head about my children: I need
them to be well and happy before I can start to relax. And I've got
to leave Levi and Ruby back here with Eszter, our au pair, tomorrow.
They love her and know her so well, and it's only for one day, but it
feels odd and uncomfortable.

And I'm anxious about what I'm going to see. How am I going to respond to Farin? Will I feel like I will want to take her home — and is that what Martin wants me to feel? But what if I don't?

But I can't pretend. God's just going to have to speak to me.

And tomorrow is going to be a new day, a new experience, a life-changing one. I'm excited about that.

Are we going to have to move here? Who knows what could happen?

★ 6 AUGUST 2007

We found out today that Prem Kiran's building a restoration center — 100 km and four hours away from Mumbai, too far for the old life to claw them back too easily — and that Farin's mother's come out of prostitution. Even better, the whole family want to move out there when it's complete.

I found something else out too today. Farin and her family are all Muslim. It makes me smile. Here I am in a Christian band, traveling the world, and God's breaking my heart over the very people that my newspaper tells me I need to be afraid of. I love his sense of humour.

We leave at 7:30 tomorrow. We'll leave our youngest two here with Eszter, but Elle, Noah and Indi will make the day's trip to Mumbai with us.

It's odd, even though we know we can't bring her home I still feel like I'm her dad. I can't pull away from that and I still feel responsible.

And I'm excited. Anna finally gets to see Farin and the project and everything that I've been living through for the last year.

♥ **7 AUGUST 2007**

It was raining when we got there. It was very muggy and hot. And it stank. There was sweat pouring down my back as we were led down these alleys – places where anyone could do anything. And I felt vulnerable, especially having the children with me.

But when I saw Farin I recognized her instantly. And I knew why all this had happened. She's so like our children – she has a picklish side to her and is attractive. I knew why Martin had felt all those feelings.

And at the same time I didn't want to take her home. I saw the way that she was with her friends and how the community was set up around her and I knew that she was being looked after and was happy and well. There was a little boy in the corner that didn't look happy and well, and my heart went out to him. But I don't think we could bring him back ... if anything we'd need to move out here to look after him. My head went there for a minute, but there are five of my own that I'm a mum to, and now pregnant with no. 6.

★ **8 AUGUST 2007**

It was everything I hoped for. Anna was blown away. She's a mum, so it's not unnatural to be in there doing her mum-type things: caring, loving, hugging, smiling, pouring out compassion from every pore. Some of all this that's coming out of her is totally natural, some of it's completely spiritual. I think she's caught it too. I think she knows that this is something we have to give our lives to.

The kids start to understand too. Elle's right in there, getting emotional, her heart broken.

"Oh Dad," she said to me as we got back in the car to take us back to the airport, "what can we do?"

Elle's right: all our conversations are going to be different from now on. Nothing will be the same. Our actions are what count most from here on in.

★ 7 OCTOBER 2007

I've been thinking about the money side of all this.

I guess I'm just worrying that all this might come off as looking like a lightweight attempt at doing something to make us feel good. This CompassionArt thing is about far more than that, but I guess there's a question that needs to be asked: what am I modeling, what signals am I sending out to people by living in luxury like this, having great holidays and guest rooms and money to spare?

I know that I'm not doing this to please the critics. I'm not doing this to impress people either. You're never going to win if you're judged on that, whatever you do.

But I just hope that people see this for the project that it is.

I hope people see the finish line.

★ 6 DECEMBER 2007

Mary-Anna Merciful was born today. She is beautiful.

Also all twelve writers now released from their deals *and* any claim to these copyrights. I'm not sure this has been done before. Just in time, as we start the retreat in four weeks.

New birth.

♥ 9 JANUARY 2008

Mary-Anna was born in December and it's been a crazy time: getting presents, sorting out rooms, menus and schedules for the retreat . . . but very exciting. And it got better when Pip (Paul's wife) and I got up to Scotland for a couple of days. They were in the middle of a feedback session, playing their songs to each other and talking about them. I felt very emotional. A little embarrassed too, but mainly just really emotional. I looked at each of their faces and knew that God was doing something amazing. So much unity, so much intensity, so much of God . . .

★ 11 JANUARY 2008

The retreat. It was . . . I don't know what it was. It was something more than I ever could have imagined. It was a family, a most amazing time of unity and openness. It was raw and risky too, and that made it even better.

And the songs! They're great. They came and nobody really remembers now who wrote what chorus or who put what ideas together for a melody or a hook. It was unity like I've never experienced before and it made all the mundane, practical stuff that filled the weeks beforehand worthwhile.

Talk to Michael and Israel and Les Moir, we need to make a record.

★ 20 FEBRUARY 2008

This is hard. I'm at Abbey Road studios and it's the first time I've been away during the school half-term holidays in years. It feels wrong somehow, and I miss the kids more than I can say. I feel like I'm letting them down. And I know that things have started to mount and build up, that Anna and I are feeling like we have had to carry something. We have to up our game here, to be better together, kinder and more supportive. It takes extra effort to do it – it's tempting just to get absorbed by the project – but if I don't share it with Anna I'm just not going to make it through in one piece.

The potential is amazing. For the first time in our lives – in a significant way – we're doing something together. The band's always been my thing, even though Anna's been involved too. But it's different now. She loves it – we've become a team. And the future will be amazing – she's a great ambassador for the charity. Even though she's not here, I know she's all over this project.

Oh, and Tomlin's just recorded the most amazing vocal for "You Have Shown Us." Words can't even get close to describing the sense of God being there in the room.

♥ **21 FEBRUARY 2008**

It's been hard this week. We've struggled at times, and just 'cause God's in it doesn't mean it's easy. Noah misses his dad. I try to play football with him in the garden, but he just looks at me in a funny way. He knows I can't play. But we just made the best of what we could.

♥ **3 MARCH 2008**

All I know is that God is changing my heart and my views on stuff that I thought I knew about, but I really have no idea. I thought I knew about poverty – I see it on the television – but I think my view was quite naïve.

★ 20 MARCH 2008

Since that last entry I've been out for a few days in Nashville, recording vocals. Toby Mac and Leeland and Andy Park came and set the place on fire, Michael smiled and Paul and Steven were complete pros.

And we think we've found a project to be involved in. Something for us to donate a big chunk of the money to. I didn't want to push too early. I wanted it to be organic and there are certain decisions that are out of my hands. I need to provide vision and leadership but there is so much need. We feel we're on to something, providing creative arts centers in places where kids would never have the chance to be creative, not only to provide primary health and education but the chance for people to be artists and creative beings. Surely this is the hallmark of CompassionArt, providing clean water and helping to answer questions that I think need asking: like where are the African record producers? Where is the Cambodian symphony orchestra? Where are the Indian worship leaders who are going to come through and travel the world with their brand of worship leading that will teach and shape the Church? We need to know the answers – maybe we can be them.

★ 3 APRIL 2008

This is real life now. I didn't know that taking on all this would have such an effect on our home life. I'm in the studio, recording this record for the mission field, but I feel like I'm neglecting my own kids. Are we really doing the right thing? Can we really carry this by ourselves?

I know this, though; that everyone, wherever they are, needs to engage with what God's put in their hands. But it's hard work. I just watched Bono on YouTube, speaking at an award ceremony from back in 2007. He talks about how all this – this helping of others and living for something better than houses and cars and nothing more – is not a burden, but an adventure.

Right now the money we've needed to fund this project has reached another level. Even if we sold everything we have and moved into a caravan we will need more than that to run the whole thing and live out the vision and the dreams for it. The question is, what can I do with the influence and the microphone – it's more important than what I can achieve by living in a caravan.

So we got our hearts broken, the idea's now bigger than us, it's hard graft time. The phone's ringing twice as much. And I've got a tax bill coming up.

♥ 3 APRIL 2008

Mart got back from Portugal last night. He's talking about Uganda, saying that he needs to know soon whether we're all going or not. It seems to me like an all or nothing thing – so we're all going. Just a whole lot of jabs to sort out now.

I'm a mother – this is my job, giving it all to my kids. And part of the sacrifice is giving Mart the space to do his thing too. And this is a privilege, even though it's hard sometimes. But just think about how great these experiences can be for the kids. . .

★ 4 APRIL 2008

I know what I'm like: I'm full of lots of ideas and I love to run with them as fast as I can. I wake up with an idea and it's in place by lunchtime. Then two weeks will go by and Anna will say that she didn't know about it – the website, the studio, the whatever. But being busy is not an excuse to forget that our greatest responsibility is to our own children.

All these plates are spinning all the time. There's no on/off button for any of them: children, school, CompassionArt, Delirious?, being at home, being away.

But the dreams keep coming. Can we really take six kids to Uganda? How many cases will we need?

RISE UP, CHURCH!

Darlene Zschech

MY HEART BREAKS AS I WRITE THIS.
SO MANY TIMES I SENSE MY PASSIONS RISE AND COME INTO FOCUS. I FIND MYSELF DETERMINED TO TAKE A STAND AGAINST INJUSTICE. THESE FEELINGS ARE STRONG, PURE AND UNCOMPROMISING. I FEEL READY TO HELP CHANGE THE WORLD.

And then there are the other days. My heart can feel clouded by so many unanswered questions. Why do so many people have to live under such crushing difficulty and despair? Why did we let injustice spread so far and so deep? What else can I do that might help to make a difference?

It is in this place that each of us can so easily find ourselves frozen in passive response to the overwhelming cry of brokenness on the planet.

But we are not created to be ice sculptures — we are not made to be cold and unfeeling and immovable. We are made to live and rage and fight and change our world.

★

My husband, Mark, and I have been wrestling with this for many years. What should our personal response be to the cries of injustice that we hear? We've tried to act and put our hands to whatever work we can, but most days we are left feeling that we fall incredibly short of doing all that we could do. It was with this kind of internal struggle that we began dreaming and talking with Martin and Anna. If the Church is made up of true worshippers, and if we understand Romans 12 and the possibilities and responsibilities that face us all, then what kind of difference could we hope to make? If we use our whole selves to give God what he deserves – not just with hands raised and a song sung with passion, but with hands outstretched, ready to work and bring answers – how much more could we achieve?

Something has been happening over the last few years. We have been learning and teaching as this unfolding revelation has become clearer before us. We have begun to wake up to what it is that God wants: our hearts lifted to heaven, our ears desperate to hear his gentle voice that leads and guides us. God is a God of purpose, and he is not looking for more gifted singers of songs. He wants – as ever – the hearts of his children to be soft, open and listening to what he is saying; that we each would take our place across the earth as his hands and his feet, bringing hope, bringing change, bringing Jesus.

There's a paradox in all of this, that God knows our failings and weakness and yet he would use us at all. Who would have thought that the very same God who made heaven and earth, the same God who flung the stars into the skies, would use *us*? And who would have thought that so much of the work he has for us is so close to where our daily lives are lived out?

I always thought being used by God to bring justice would mean being sent to the farthest corners of the earth with nothing much more than used tea bags being sent over to us to keep us going on. But I don't see things that way now. Our mission fields often lie much closer to home, in our neighborhoods, our schools, the areas where we might have even the slightest bit of influence — as well as those far-flung countries. The truth is that the compass that points to where God sends us responds to one thing only: need. Where there is pain and suffering, loneliness and grief, hunger and oppression, that is where God's people are drawn, near and far — each and every one of us.

♥

There is so much that I wrestle with when it comes to the plight of much of the world. The poverty experienced hourly by thousands of people is more crushing and devastating than I think I could ever really understand. The fact that each year 2.2 million children die from diseases we routinely immunize against in the West, that 1.4 million lose their lives every year because their drinking water is not clean and they have no access to proper sanitation, that half the world's children live in poverty. Almost 30 percent of all children in developing countries are thought to be underweight or stunted, and nearly a billion people entered the twenty-first century unable to read or write their names. Half the world's population must try to sustain life on less than $2 per day.*

The fact that I live in a nation that is extremely blessed and rich seems so radically unfair. And even when I choose to live with the increasing understanding of responsibility, the death toll rises as yet another 25,000–30,000 children will die within the next twenty-four hours simply because they do not have the money to prevent poverty from robbing them of their lives.

But in the middle of all this — all these thoughts and feelings and stirrings — I know that there is justice. I know that Jesus' grace and

* All from www.globalissues.org/

love leads him to see all people as equal no matter what their circumstances, regardless of whether they are rich or poor. Justice levels mountains and puts right the greatest wrongs in society and is the great defining line of truth when it comes to the treatment of humanity: without it, the people perish.

When I was a little girl I was given some amazing examples of what justice looked like in the flesh. My parents and others in the church took food and clothing to a group of extremely poor children, most of whom were orphaned. This was the good news of Jesus in flesh and blood. This was what justice looked like: simple, practical, personal. It was modeled for me beautifully by these wonderful Christians who put their faith into action.

Social justice is the outworking of this revelation, serving those unfairly treated, in a practical way. And if I may speak honestly, I believe that it is our role as Christians to see that no person is disadvantaged, and that every person has access to the good news. We cannot ignore it; we cannot take the ostrich position and pray that the problems will go away or that someone else will fix it. I actually believe that this could be the Church's finest hour *if* we get serious about finding ways to align with others and make headway with bringing a solution.

That *if* is a big one. For so many of us it means overcoming a culture that tells us to serve only ourselves and grow nothing more than our bank accounts. But the journey of worship and justice continues to grow in strength and clarity, and although we are just beginning to scratch the surface, we are at least on the way. Churches are getting the idea and signing up an army of workers to change the world. Willow Creek – a huge church in the USA – has an incredible organization that is fighting HIV/AIDS, and works with the experts on the ground. In Papua New Guinea, there is a church whose whole mission is to supply and drive fully equipped ambulances, and then take the equipment into remote slums and villages to bring medicines, doctors and much-needed training for those again affected with HIV. Hundreds of churches across the earth have partnered with child sponsorship programs that are the experts on the ground within poverty-stricken environments. Working through local churches, these groups are bringing help where it is needed most. This list could go on and on.

It's been amazing to see how different aspects of the global Church have always made the fight against injustice their theme song. But we're kidding ourselves if we think that we've led the way on this. We haven't. To our shame, secular society has led the charge. Even though I received criticisms for it, I still wholeheartedly stand behind the work of people such as Geldof and Bono. In fact, the global music industry has done a lot for many years when it comes to making the average person even marginally aware of what is going on today in our world. So have Bill and Melinda Gates and the many government bodies who have poured millions upon millions of dollars into aid and development. These are the ones who have picked up the baton we have dropped. These are the ones whose work has plugged the gaps that we have left. These are the ones who have carried out God's wishes, even though they might not have been aware of it.

Why should there be so much criticism towards great men and women with large enough hearts to take their energy, wisdom and finance to those who could truly benefit from it? Surely, if we agree that we are all created in the image of God, it must be true that people who don't profess a faith can be tapping into God's purpose and passion. Could this be what it means for the rocks to cry out – for elements that seem so set against him to be caught up in God's miraculous plans to put right the wrongs of a fallen world?

It is not too late for the Church to work against poverty again. So much more time and money and energy and risk is needed. In fact, I thank God for anyone who is championing the cries of the seemingly forgotten, the orphans and the widows, the many women who literally bear the brunt of the outfall of poverty.

We as the Church have much catching up to do, and many lessons to learn. We need to work not so that we can feel good or feed our egos, but simply because the need remains so great.

The good news is, there is not one church leader I have talked to around the world whose heart is not gripped by the mountain of need we are all faced with. I believe the word of God makes the call to our mission plain and simple; all we need to do is to get busy doing it.

There are armies of people, all across the earth, who are ready to go, ready to serve, ready to bring finance and expertise, energy, hope and love wherever they can. This is the Church at its most beautiful; looking out, looking up, strongest when serving, boldest when following. She is at her finest when seen with outstretched hands, taking on the stance of service.

Look hard enough and you will see her in action, taking food and blankets to the cold and hungry, fostering the children in our own communities who have been left to a life called "survival of the fittest." She's in action when congregations push themselves and give more than they could get away with in order to provide clean water to a village, or become a church that fosters another church in the developing world. I saw this in action in a project we were involved with in 2006: HopeRwanda. Hundreds of churches used the skills of their people – their teachers, builders, surgeons and so on – to simply come alongside and serve the people in whatever it was they required.

Each of us can do something, however small or large that may be.

It might be a seemingly impossible mountain of dire poverty to tear down, but our small acts combined can do it. We have said for far too long that the problem is too big, that we are unable to make a difference. But while this might make a comfortable space in which we can ignore the guilt and get on with serving ourselves, it does nothing for our faith, or our souls. With all my heart, I encourage you to be a good steward of where you will spend your time, energy and finance to help. But don't judge the poor, or the many levels of what poverty is, or how the poor became the poor. If it is in your power to help, then help.

★

To even slightly understand the effect of injustice and poverty, you've got to let it touch you, let it affect you. Almost everybody feels compassion, but it takes personal leadership to move to action. The greatest example? Jesus himself. When he started with his declaration that the "spirit of the Lord was upon him," it wasn't just a neat reference back to an ancient scripture. Over the years that followed it was clear that his life was carried out in view of the poor, that he was affected, impacted and disturbed by a world scarred by so much pain and suffering.

It is time for the Church to truly rise and shine. We need to not just talk about bringing change and changing the world, but to radically roll up our sleeves and get ourselves fueled with serving others.

Can we do it?

In my heart of hearts the answer I want to give is *yes*, but there is a cost. We will be required to lay down our own agendas – maybe in a way that we never have before. This is not beyond us, Church. If we will make up our minds to keep on breaking down the walls that have traditionally separated us — walls of prejudice or misunderstanding or ignorance or even just plain old fear — then the future could be utterly different from the present. How exciting is that?

♥

Worst of all poverty is the poverty of hope. Not having anything to hope or believe in simply drains the body of life. In East Africa there's a recurring phenomenon they call *idle*. Young men and women living in such extreme poverty wake up and have nowhere to go, nothing to do. So they simply sit still and preserve body fuel. With no promise of change coming, any sense of hope that remains soon evaporates.

A friend put it this way: poverty may affect a child, but poverty is never born in a child. Poverty steals hope . . . and that is the greatest poverty of all.

On one of our trips to Rwanda I got to watch doctors carry out open-heart surgery on one very sick woman. A great team of surgeons had gathered for ten days to help relieve the burgeoning number of those needing radical medical intervention in order to stay alive. To be honest, I was totally captivated by the miracle I was witnessing, and being able to watch the blood flow back through the heart after just a small amount of time was exhilarating. I asked the head surgeon whether there were any differences operating on people in the developing world compared to those back home: "So, when you get inside a person, what are the differences?" He told me that in countries marked by poverty he never has to cut through fat, just flesh and muscle. Back in the West, the operations are needed to combat the excesses of life, rather than the lack of it. Apart from that, he said, we are all pretty much the same.

The next day I sat with a woman who was very sick with AIDS. She was breastfeeding her little baby. I was shocked: why would she put her baby at such risk? One of the workers explained that, without medicines, the lady's choices were horrific and stark: does she feed the baby and allow it to live a little longer, or does she starve the child to try to prevent it from becoming infected, only to be orphaned anyway?

I went back to my hotel and was physically sick as I was challenged to my core. Just being in that hotel room left me feeling like a hypocrite, and again I felt so helpless, yet so charged with a passion that is furiously unrelenting when it comes to finding answers. I know all too well that I am no expert and that I could do so much more, yet surely that does not disqualify me from taking up the fight for my brothers and sisters who are perishing? Why should mothers have to feed their kids on mud in the hope that the soil will trick their bodies into thinking they have eaten something nutritious – or at least calm the hunger that rages, for just a short while?

There was another trip – this time to the rubbish dumps of Cambodia. It was there that I saw mothers having to put their own two-year-olds to work, at the risk of them being stolen for prostitution or killed by dumper trucks whose drivers do not see the little ones searching for enough recyclable rubbish to earn a few cents a day. If things worked well for them then their combined efforts would earn enough for the family to afford to eat small amounts to survive, and to pay the pimp of the trash heap his fee for allowing them to be there.

There are mothers in India who are forced to rent out their newborns to beggars, who drug the children so that they will be drowsy and less trouble when they weave in and out of the cars that wait at traffic lights.

There are girls who are tricked, sold or stolen and taken across borders where they are forced to work as prostitutes. The lucky ones escape, but who can return home when such shame follows close behind?

Darlene Zschech **49**

There are children who are forced to become soldiers, whose training requires that they kill family members. Again, there is no prospect of returning home after such horrors.

Workers, paid next to nothing, forced into unsafe factories. Small children, with their tiny hands, are forced to reach into complex machines, risking amputation and death as they polish cutting tools or needles.

Communities forced to drink stagnant water because the nearest fresh-water well has been taken over by lawless rebels, who rape any women making the journey there with their empty buckets and bowls.

Farmers, whose soil could feed a family if only the rains would come or the floods would stop, or if the price of what they sell was fair enough.

Families who – for the price of one of our cinema tickets – could start their own business that would provide enough income to lift them out of the type of poverty that threatens to rob them of life.

How did we let the world get like this?

How did we stay silent?

How can we not rage against it?

★

What have I got to bring? It's a question we all ask ourselves. But the answer does not need to be long, nor is it hard to come up with. We have all been given gifts, talents, relationships, ideas, finance. Used strategically, with our church, or with great leadership, then there is no limit to what we can do.

The reality is that this is a matter of the greatest urgency, and we need to approach this uncomfortable truth, both locally and globally, intelligently and swiftly. We must work with experts, and then, fueled by prayer and unity – not trying to reinvent the wheel, but working together for the greater cause of restoring the godly value of a human life – we must serve the world in need.

I have been reading and consuming information on possible solutions. I've been trying to become educated on these subjects that have torn at my heart. I have very limited knowledge, but from all that I have found out to date it is clear that change is going to take an army of people, not just one particular group being invigorated for a season or even a lifetime. If we all truly believe that everyone is in this together, then we must all play our part in the healing process on every level. It means not worrying about who is getting credit; it means doing without so that others may have the basic essentials that sustain life. It means making being uncomfortable a reasonable place to live, and I believe it means becoming more confident than we've ever been. We can all do something. We *must* all do something. In fact, this generation can be the generation who stand up to say *enough is enough*. We can be the ones who scream the message, in words and actions, that this level of inequality ends here.

We can do it. We can change this world. As some wise lady once said: never doubt that a small group of committed people can change the world; indeed, it is the only thing that ever has.

We can – we are – the hope that the world so desperately needs. If not us, then who? If not now, then when?

Rise up, people!

Rise up, Church!

TOWELS AND SOCKS

Chris Tomlin

WE'RE IN A TOWNSHIP OUTSIDE CAPE TOWN, SOUTH AFRICA. IT'S THE END OF OUR TIME IN THE TIN-ROOFED BUILDING. OUR VISIT HAS SHOWN US WHAT LOCAL CHRISTIANS ARE DOING TO PUT THEIR FAITH INTO ACTION AMONG SOME OF THE POOREST PEOPLE I'VE EVER SAT WITH. I HAVE THESE KIDS STANDING AROUND ME, ALL DIAMOND SMILES AND FADED WESTERN T-SHIRTS, EACH ONE OF THEM WANTING ME TO TAKE A PHOTO OF THEM AND SHOW THEM WHAT THEY LOOK LIKE ON THE LITTLE SCREEN. THEN THIS MUM COMES OUT — A LADY WHO LOOKS TEN YEARS OLDER THAN ME BUT WHO I'M GUESSING IS PROBABLY A FEW YEARS YOUNGER. SHE GETS CLOSER AND I CAN SEE HER EYES HAVE A LOOK ABOUT THEM THAT IS LOADED WITH STORIES AND SORROW. THE KIDS' SMILES SEEM TO FADE FROM MY VIEW AND THE NOISE BACKS OFF. THE MUM PULLS A BABY ROUND FROM THE SLING THAT WAS HIDING IT BEHIND HER BACK.

"Please take my baby."

Her words rob me of my own. She carries on looking at me, her eyes filling in the gaps left by the silence that has fallen. She wants me to take her baby — and I don't even know whether it's a boy or a girl — she wants me to take it back to America, desperate to give it a chance, as if being without the woman who gave it life will be better than the fate that remains for it out here.

"Please take my baby."

I can't stand it. I can't stand this level of hopelessness. I can't deal with these kids being ill, being born into a life that offers nothing more than disease and tragedy. I look back at the mum and her child and then at the others. I'm finding it unnerving to see this kind of hopelessness that rests on a child born HIV-positive; I find it painful to know that so many diseases are raging through the continent simply because there is not enough clean water. This is poverty with no way out, poverty without hope. Poverty that means the baby probably won't live beyond five years old.

"Please take my baby."

♥

It's easy to get wrapped up in what you want to accomplish in life. From the first days of school we're setting targets and working out plans to reach a certain goal by a certain time. We're figuring out ways of getting further faster, or landing the lifestyle that we want. And each of these are OK: there's nothing all that wrong with wanting your life to look a certain way, nothing all that wrong with ambitions – apart from the simple fact that this isn't the way it is for most other people around the world. All our planning and dreaming about what great things we can aim for is based on the fact that there's a decent chance that we might just be able to pull it off. We've got the tools, we've got the opportunities; most of the time the question for us is whether we've got the determination or the guts to pull it off. Ambition for us is a form of hope that has been fed on the assumption that we will get what we want.

But when you're standing in borrowed clothes pleading with a stranger to take your baby back with him to America, life is starved of opportunity. Hope has all but vanished. Hope has little to offer.

For those people around the world whose poverty is held in place by the absence of hope and opportunity, life is crushing. It's harder than I could ever imagine, bleaker and grayer. Without hope of things changing, what is there to keep you going? When there are 600 of you sharing one water tap, or there are six of you sleeping in a space the size of the average Westerner's wardrobe, or you have been exposed to rape and violence and been forced to flee your home ... where's the hope?

We Christians talk a lot about hope. And it's right and good that we do. We have hope in Christ — hope that this life will be filled with purpose, that the things we do wrong can be forgiven, that our Father and Creator knows and loves us, that after we die we will be united with him. But while all this is true, we can't close our eyes to the way that life really is for millions of the poorest people around the world. We can't ignore the fact that for some of our neighbors on this planet, life lacks hope.

Some of us need to open our eyes to this and wake up. We need to allow our hearts to get stirred, to be made to feel awkward and uncomfortable, to rage against the injustice of a situation where hope cannot feed, protect or heal.

Others of us have been stirred and moved and have shed some tears, but we need to act. We need to wake up to the fact that we are responsible, that we have to do something. There is a time to pray and a time to sing, a time to weep and a time to laugh. There is never a time to turn our back on poverty.

So we need God's compassion inside us. All of us do. We need to be made less comfortable, not more, to be more stirred up, not less. In this upside-down world we need to learn to walk the right way up.

WHAT ABOUT WORSHIP?

I find myself amazed at the way that music has always been an incredible part of what people know about God. I joke a lot with my pastor back home about what people remember most: the songs or the message. The truth, some of the time, is that when they're walking back out to their cars it's the songs and the melodies that often get into their hearts and heads. This might mean that the musicians feel as if they score a few points against their pastors, but it's a heavy responsibility: what are we actually getting people to sing? What are we writing about? Are we teaching people correctly about the things that God is passionate about? Are we reflecting what he wants from us? Are we singing about the truth, or are our lyrics just another collection of nice rhymes but little else?

Tackling poverty and preparing to sing our worship out to God are linked. Music's power makes it possible for it to connect to our emotions, and despite the fact that some people might tell us to calm them down, I'm pretty sure that when it comes to the Christian response to poverty and injustice we need to be as emotional as possible. If we denied our God-given emotions it would be like eating a meal without being able to taste it or sitting through a film with your eyes closed. God deals in emotions: he doesn't deny them.

There's something about worship and singing that, even in the worst of times, brings freedom. You can see it with Paul and Silas, two guys who have been beaten for their faith, who are talking about a man unlike any other who has saved the people, and they get arrested, battered and put in the bottom of the dungeon and chained up for their faith. And if it were me, I'd probably be complaining. I'd be feeling sorry for myself, reminding God how I'd done so much for him yet by way of return I'd ended up beaten, my face bloodied, perhaps with a broken arm, bruises all over and sitting chained and wasting away in a dungeon. Yet what do you find them doing? Worshipping God.

Worship brings freedom. We see it in more recent history too. The slavery issue has been huge where I come from in the US. Yet out of those chains and shadeless plantation fields have come some of the greatest songs that have gone on to shape the music of America and beyond. At times out of extreme oppression and poverty can come songs of freedom, songs of hope. As Rich Mullens pointed out, to sing about God is the most reiterated command of scripture. More than all the things we are told to do, singing is the activity that we are told to devote ourselves to.

No one can take away a song from you. They can take everything, but they can't take a song. I love Psalm 40: it's such a perfect scripture for the message of this CompassionArt project:

> I waited patiently for the LORD . . .

and this "me" could be any of us – from any country, any background and any horrors or hardships, born into the depths of poverty, born into this really unfair world – if we wait patiently for the Lord then at some point we will be able to say what follows:

> . . . he turned to me and heard my cry.
> He lifted me out of the slimy pit,
> out of the mud and mire;
> he set my feet on a rock
> and gave me a firm place to stand.
> He put a new song in my mouth,

a hymn of praise to our God.

Many will see and fear

and put their trust in the LORD.

Psalm 40:1–3

Even out of all this, even out of the mud and the mire, he lifts us out and puts a song in our mouths. A new song. I think it's interesting that David says it's a new song; maybe our songs get stale, maybe they get a little out of tune: maybe we need to ask God for that new song.

And just as we need to ask for the new songs, we need to be the ones coming up with the lifestyles that lift others out of the mud and mire – that's the kind of ambition that I think God loves best. Just as the songs of the slaves needed the physical freedom that came with the emancipation proclamation, so too do our songs need our actions alongside them. We must sing about freedom and hope with all that we have, and do all that we can to see that our hands help to provide it for those living with too little hope. We must sing and we must get involved.

GETTING INVOLVED

I didn't have to pray about whether to get involved in this CompassionArt project.

When the e-mail came through I remember the thoughts that followed: that this is something we have been talking about in my world for quite some time, that this is one of those situations where whatever platform I have can be used completely for good. At the end of my days I don't want to look back and see that I've taken whatever influence I've had and just used it to promote songs; I want to know that

I've been given to really reach the last and the least of those who breathe this same air and live under this same sun as me.

It wasn't something I had to pray about.

I hope that this whole thing is a starting point, the first step to something far bigger, not just a single story about a single album that lives on a shelf. How come? Well, this has not been an easy venture to set up; it's one thing to get twelve people together to write a record, but to have the publishers and the record companies and the lawyers all come together and support it, and give all the royalties away and put their heart behind it as well . . . there's something about it that makes me think this surely is a God kingdom thing. So I'm hoping that it doesn't stop with the album but that it goes out to influence others: other artists, other creatives, other people with office jobs or time on their hands and a heart that starts to beat a little faster when they think about the gap between rich and poor that exists all around us.

The unity's the thing. As songwriters, we're all in this together – nobody really knows who did what to what song, and nobody's claiming any of the work as their own. And that's a different experience for me: I've always written songs by myself; then if I need some help I'll just ask a friend. But something new has happened with this way of working together, something that's been reminding me constantly of the last prayer that we know Jesus prayed:

> I pray also for those who will believe in me through their message, that all of them may be one, Father, just as you are in me and I am in you. May they also be in us so that the world may believe that you have sent me. I have given them the glory that you gave me, that they may be one as we are one: I in them and you in me. May they be brought to

complete unity to let the world know that you sent me and have loved them even as you have loved me.

John 17:20–23

Every one of us is encouraged to live for the personal, to put unity second and our individual concerns first. But that's not the way it's supposed to be. That's not the way it is in the kingdom of God.

Kingdoms are strange concepts for us Americans. We live in a collection of states, a country made up of many leaders representing many people. But to live in a kingdom . . . that means there must be a king, someone who is the head of it all. I know that someone to be the Son of God and I believe that Jesus is head of this kingdom. He's the one that's driving it, he's setting the pace and creating a truly upside-down way of doing things. I'm pretty sure that in most kingdoms throughout the world and through time, the subjects would be asked to die for the king. But that's not the way God's kingdom works — the roles get switched. It's the king who died for us, and he dies for all the common people and all the subjects and all of us. That's upside down.

God left so much in our hands: even his very Spirit to give power and wisdom. And I believe that we are going to need it even more — as if we don't desperately need God's power and wisdom enough already. I believe he is coming again, this king we are talking about is coming again, this king who died for us. But he's not coming to die for us again, he's coming to set up this kingdom in full. That's when this world will be made right, but until that day I think it's broken. From what I read of scripture there are not a lot of roses coming, there are a lot of thorns. But does that mean we give up? No! We are here to share this message, here to put this love into action, here to surround ourselves with the mess and the pain of the world in order that God might transform it.

Everything about this kingdom is upside down, unlike any kingdom that has ever been known on earth. And while I believe that the Bible teaches that one day, when Jesus sets it up, this will be the final kingdom, the kingdom of all ages, still we can be a part of it today. Jesus prayed, "Let your kingdom come, let your will be done on earth as it is in heaven" and with every act of compassion and selfless living we get to advance this beautiful upside-down kingdom of God. It"s quite a privilege.

And it's quite a responsibility. In this kingdom where the usual rules don't quite seem to apply, there seems to be a special role carved out for those who follow the king. We get to carry out some of his most important tasks, regardless of how high or low our status is. We get to defend widows, feed orphans, protect the weak and fight on behalf of the poor. And here's the most awesome bit of it all: there is no Plan B. We, the Church – God's people – are his Plan A. When it comes to building God's kingdom, it's up to us. We are the hope of the world. Governments are going to fail – they may have good intentions, but those who run them are all too often fueled by a greed for power. No, it's you and me who hold all the cards, it's through us that hope is going to be taken out into the broken and starving world.

Jesus was right when he said: "In this world you will have trouble . . ." (John 16:33). This world was set right and we screwed up. This is a fallen and broken place, one where too many children and too many parents and too many strangers will die before you reach the end of this chapter. This is a world scarred by injustice. But Jesus was just as right when he went on to say: "But take heart! I have overcome the world" (John 16:33).

We serve a king who will, who does and who has overcome this broken world. It all happened on the worst ever day in history. Imagine Mary watching her son's tortured body hung up on the cross, everything she ever dreamed of suddenly reduced to a lifeless, bloodied corpse.

But the canvas that God was painting on was huge that day. Now it's possible to see the cross as the greatest thing that has ever happened for any and all of us. For the child born HIV-positive, for the man being paid a few coins a day for backbreaking work in unsafe conditions, for the girl tricked and then forced into prostitution, for the child forced to kill his brother by rebel soldiers, for the mother who offers her baby to the stranger – there is a hope.

And that hope comes from God.

And that hope is to be delivered through ordinary, unimpressive, messed-up people just like you and me.

And that hope has also found its way out to the hearts and hands of those who don't necessarily follow the king. God puts his spirit of mercy and compassion in all kinds of people, those who believe and those who don't. As God made people in his image, we all share in the DNA that has the potential to drive us out beyond ourselves to a world in need. We can all get involved.

A FEW WORDS ABOUT THOSE TOWELS AND SOCKS

Everyone makes fun of university students, particularly here in the USA. These poor college students, with too much time on their hands and no real money to do anything that's of any worth to the rest of society ... it's a myth. Living in America, earning even a minimal wage makes you way more wealthy than most people in the world. Their potential is larger than many would dream it is, and when you begin to tell them the story of how doing something now doesn't mean giving up their cell phone or handing back their iPod then something magical follows.

It's been a little over a decade now that I've been involved with a group called Passion. It's a movement among college and university students in the US and increasingly all around the world. With Louie Giglio leading, over this past year we have started to test what other simple ways our ordinary, messed-up, hope-soaked lives can be used to help with the work of this upside-down kingdom of God.

These college students are doing so many amazing things that are too numerous and vast to mention in a single chapter, but even just one story can give you a flavor of the potential they're waking up to.

We've started a campaign called Do Something Now, and it's amazing to see what happens when you challenge people who are just starting to shape their lives the way they want them. Get a theater filled with university students and tell them about the need that exists out beyond the doors, tell them that they can do something right now, and the results are a beautiful thing to see.

Louie found out that, of all the needs of all the homeless charities working in cities across America, towels and socks were way up there. I guess it's not the easiest thing to raise money for, and it wasn't on my mind until he told me all about it. It seems that towels and socks are what these charities keep on giving out, and what they need all year round. So, in the spirit of doing something now, the Passion conferences added a new part of the registration process for our events: when people come up and get their badges they also hand over the towels and socks they have brought along with them. Within a few hours the pile grows bigger and by the time we're singing and giving our worship up to God through song, a truck will be loaded full of thousands of these essential items: practical, tangible signs that God's people are learning new ways of expressing their love for him.

We're just working out that we have a choice as Christians. We could sit here and sing songs and feel good about ourselves, or we could do something better, something bigger, something more. So every conference we do, you have to bring towels and socks to give away when you register. In a few days these scrappy students solve some of the most urgent needs for those working with the homeless throughout the city.

And this is what the upside-down kingdom looks like: a bunch of people who have yet to really make anything of themselves end up changing the world.

THE END?

Politics matters, but politics is personal. We don't get to change the world by electing the right leaders — where on earth in the Bible do we ever get the idea that God wants us to outsource our action? No, we change this earth and build this kingdom with our own hands, under God's direction. The hope of the world is these true rebels, these true followers of a different way, the opposite of everything in the way the world turns, this upside-down kingdom that welcomes us all.

But some of us don't know it to be like this. We might have grown up in a Christian home or made some kind of vague noises about following God, but it's never really connected with us, never really made sense or made that much of a difference in our lives. I think we face a choice when we're like that: do we want to stand before God and say, "Look at this, all the stuff I collected, all the noise I made"?

Or do we want to lay it all down and say, "This is the time you gave me, and it went by so fast, like a click, and I spent it on the right things"?

★

And we're all standing there in the township near Cape Town.

And the mum's still pleading with us to take her child.

And we can't take it, we know that.

But there's a feeling warming up within me that says we can do something better. We can unite, we can sing and then live out the new songs that encourage us to draw together our wealth and our time and our influence and make life better — make it just that bit more bearable by degrees — until our hope becomes her own, until her world begins to turn upside down and life returns to her eyes again.

JOURNEYS WITHOUT A PASSPORT

Matt Redman

WHEN I WAS GROWING UP IT SEEMED LIKE THE POOR MADE IT INTO OUR CHURCH ABOUT TWICE A YEAR. WE DIDN'T ACTUALLY INVITE THEM THROUGH THE DOORS, BUT FOR A COUPLE OF SUNDAYS WE'D PAUSE WHAT WE USUALLY DID AND DIRECT OUR THOUGHTS TOWARD THOSE WITH LESS THAN OURSELVES. IN OCTOBER WE'D BRING OUR TINS OF BEANS AND PACKETS OF DRIED BISCUITS FOR HARVEST FESTIVAL, WHILE AT CHRISTMAS WE'D EACH OFFER UP AN OLD SHOEBOX CONTAINING AN UNWANTED TOY. ON EACH OCCASION, AFTER WE'D TAKEN OUR OFFERINGS UP TO THE FRONT, WE'D THEN SIT BACK IN THE PEWS HAPPY IN THE KNOWLEDGE THAT OUR GIFTS WERE GOING TO HELP LOCAL PEOPLE WHO DIDN'T HAVE QUITE AS MUCH MONEY AS WE DID.

And that was it.

Then it seemed we'd forget about issues of poverty until the next October or December came around. And when they did, we'd go through the whole ritual again, once more stopping the singing and the sermons, and take our tins and packets and boxes up to the front before returning to our seats.

I exaggerate a little – for one thing I grew up in a very generous church, and when I was a little older I discovered that every year they gave away a large percentage of their finances to different ministries around the world. But my point is that somehow, growing up as a

Matt Redman **71**

young boy very involved with church, the poor never really made it on to my radar screen. It was a fantastic church – but there and then it seemed that in so many of our churches we just never let poverty get past the front door and into the pulpit. As a result it was a while before I really started to connect with God's heart for the poor, and our responsibility as the Church to demonstrate that heart.

Of course, I knew that there were other churches out there: places where poverty and justice, action and activism were all part of the furniture. But to be honest, out of sheer ignorance I didn't really like those kinds of churches. Their people scared me. They were often so aggressive, so focused on their crusade, that I thought they all just needed to take it easy and stop getting quite so worked up.

And then I went to California.

I was there because a whole load of us in the Church of England had been shaken up by the Vineyard movement. This was back in the 1980s, and the thing that most impacted me was their way of worshipping with music: it was a fresh expression, a new style that went beyond the fun songs we'd been bouncing along to for a few years before then. There was something so startling about those Vineyard songs – they were charged with the idea of encounter with a living, breathing, loving heavenly Father. It had made a massive impact in my life and I grabbed the first chance I got to visit their home territory.

Vineyard's hub church back then was in Anaheim, California. The trip out was everything I hoped it would be, but there was more to it than wish fulfillment. I saw something that totally confused me. There was a large – and I mean Disney-sized large – warehouse next to the main church building. I asked what it was for – what other purpose could all that space serve if it wasn't to gather Christians together to worship God with those amazing songs? I was told that this was the home for their Mercy Ministry: their work among the local people gripped by poverty. They sent soup kitchens out from there, they clothed people and did a whole load of amazing stuff, all in the name of their faith. It left me confused: why weren't they celebrating it? Why weren't they making a bigger deal out of it all? Why wasn't this a part of their singing?

Later I would understand that there was no gap between the worship that put clothes on the homeless person's back and the worship that sent songs of love and devotion out into the atmosphere. But back then I was so narrow in my thinking that I couldn't see worship as anything other than chords, melodies and glorious harmonies arcing their way to heaven as the sun set.

SLOWLY, WE'RE WAKING UP

Things are different these days. Over the last six or seven years so many churches have woken up to one of the most urgent calls to worship that God puts before us – that we in the Church learn to put into flesh and blood what we know to be God's heart for the poor. It's more than a song, it's living, breathing actions, hard-won sacrifice and everyday service.

These days there are times when I wonder how it could be that I never even saw this as being such a vital part of my faith. How did I manage to grow up reading my Bible but somehow missing the fact that there are places where every other verse is dragging me back to the theme of how God cares for the poor? How come I glossed over this? It scares me.

And it excites me too – not the blindness, but the way that the mist and fog are clearing so rapidly these days. It seems to me that what's happening now is that all those lessons we learned about having meetings filled with songs of worship are not at all wasted – but that they're now fusing with the glorious sights and sounds that come from other acts of worship. Both are valid. When we take the passion for the melodies and the declarations of intent and apply them to fixing the injustice and oppression we see around us . . . let's just say that there's a lot of potential.

We're learning that while there are different streams of the Church that excel in different expressions of the kingdom of God, it's possible – and indeed healthy – for every church to aim to have a little piece of everything. One community's strongest point may be its preaching, but they'll also have a heart for the poor. We're learning to aim for the whole pie, not just settling for a single slice of it. We want to know what it is that the kingdom of God is all about. We want to know what it looks and smells like, how it gets demonstrated, and then to see how it can all be lived out in the flesh and blood of our own lives.

It's Acts 2 all over – the Church that breaks bread together, prays together, reads together, preaches together and shares all that they have together. When our churches start to look like that you know that something special can't be far off.

THREE TRIPS: A LIFETIME OF EXPERIENCE

It took a long time for me to get from being confused in Anaheim. Meeting unforgettable people and getting forced out of my comfort zone speeded up the process. Like the day I turned twenty-one. It was my first time in South Africa and I found myself in a township called Inanda in Kwa Zulu Natal.

I wasn't ready for the drive. Being behind all that glass and metal, just meters away from such poverty as I had never seen before, going too fast to talk with anyone, but slow enough to see the suffering that veiled their eyes ... it messed me up. I'd previously only ever seen these sights on TV, but now being there myself – yet still one step removed – increased the sense of discomfort dramatically.

We stopped. Meeting people in a local church was better than feeling like an air-conditioned tourist. These people I met – Christians who were doing the helping and others who were being helped – confused me. There they were, with next to nothing, yet treating those of us who had arrived for a two-hour visit with more generosity than I had ever seen in my life. How could they be capable of giving so much when they clearly had so little?

And then I began to work out what else I was feeling. Fear. These people were looking at me kind of funny and I really couldn't tell what they were thinking. I was far from home – no phone, no sense of direction, no resources that would be worth that much out there – and I was scared. Had my life of comfort and security really created such a barrier against poverty and suffering? Was I really so out of my depth in this situation? What did it say about my faith?

I felt the same when I visited a leper colony in Mumbai. I'm over-cautious about blood, hospitals, health and hygiene at the best of times, so this visit was always going to be a challenge.

Mumbai's a crowded city to say the least, one that cannot hide its poverty any more than it can neutralize its smells or quiet its car horns. But when you get 7,000 people living below an overpass, breathing in air saturated with the fog of traffic fumes – 7,000 people living as outcasts and rejects, objects of fear and hatred – it's hard not to have a reaction. Again I was scared. I knew that there's a treatment for leprosy, that you can't catch it by touch, but the knowledge doesn't seem to do much good when you're walking around and seeing people with feet, hands or part of faces shriveled up or wasting away.

I didn't want to be a spectator or come back with an "I've Been to a Leper Colony" souvenir badge. I wanted to connect with people and have it change me. It was then that I felt God challenge me. The only way I was going to get over all this fear and hesitation was to walk up and embrace someone. The only way I was going to get over my fear was to feel it.

He was an old guy. He was wasting away and it took no more than one glance to know how ill he was. The eyes – they told the suffering by their glaze, dulled to life by too much sorrow. But joy wasn't too far beneath the surface for this man. He was friendly but couldn't speak English. I suppose that's why the embrace was important – it was the only way to cross the boundary. I don't think I left a whole lot behind, but I know that God did a whole lot in me.

The choice was similar when we were on a trip to Cape Town. We were in a township and it was the first time that I had met someone who was clearly infected with AIDS. It was the same thing – the same choice: either you stand on the other side of the room and observe or you try to connect, you try to get involved.

A lot of us have a notion that we could get involved with a homeless ministry or a missions trip, but it's the fears that stop us – fear for our safety, fear that we are completely inadequate, fear that we might say the wrong thing or forget to do the right thing or just freeze completely. And perhaps it's OK to feel inadequate – perhaps we don't all have to be experts, perhaps we don't have to have all the solutions before we join in.

So all these experiences that I've been privileged enough to soak up in Africa or India have started to teach me something – a lesson that others have worked out long ago and without the air miles: that our comfort zones need to be challenged, that fear is not a barrier to action, that our choice to get involved with those whose lives are scarred by poverty is not one we take because we have all the answers or because we can fix the problems – but because we were not made to live in isolation.

There aren't many of us who would have to drive more than an hour to find people living in poverty. Most of us could reach their homes in a few minutes. There aren't many cities in the world that don't have homeless people and there are very few communities that don't have individuals who are lonely or outcast, overlooked or ignored by the rest of us. And what's my point? That none of us is unable to have our comfort zones challenged by experiencing poverty face to face.

SOMETHING TO HANG ALL THIS ON

The experiences themselves were a large part of my journey from skeptic to convert, but they weren't the sole vehicle. I needed the biblical teaching to hang the experiences on. Without the teaching I've heard on the issue of poverty and the potential that the Church has to change the situation, I'm just another guy who's been stirred up.

It's when you start to figure out what God has to say about all this that the journey really begins making sense.

There's a verse in Proverbs (19:17) that turned my world upside down. It shocks me every time I read it. It says:

> He who is kind to the poor lends to the LORD,
> and he will reward him for what he has done.

It's a profoundly controversial verse. We think of someone to whom we lend as being less than us – a debtor. But does this really mean that we can give God anything at all? Isn't everything his anyway?

And isn't it the case that the whole narrative of scripture is about the otherness of God, the self-sufficiency of God, the fact that he is not in our debt at all? Isn't scripture soaked in the truth that everything in the earth is his, that he gives life and breath, that he's not made by human hands, that he doesn't need anything from us? And then this verse comes along. And it shocks me. Here's this self-sufficient God, this debtor of no man. OK, so perhaps he does owe us a couple of things – death and judgement – but what this says seems for a brief tiny moment here to go right against the grain I'd assumed ran deep through time itself.

I've spent the last five years preaching on the otherness of God. I've tried to write songs around it too, drawing out the idea that God is independent and we are dependent, that God is self-sufficient but that we are insufficient without him – yet this is the only verse in scripture that doesn't fit in.

How it all fits together theologically I don't know. But I'm sure that the verse is there to shock and jolt us, and to show that giving to the poor is not just another line on a checklist. It's actually something rated extremely highly in God's eyes.

Perhaps I need to rethink my view of things. I grew up so centered around bringing songs of worship to God. I never even conceived in my mind that God might tell me to go away, that my songs might be displeasing, a mark of hypocrisy undermined by my lifestyle. Yet Amos 5 makes it clear that even the most polished worshippers are repulsive to God if their lives trample on the poor and allow injustice and oppression to flourish.

There's a whole hymn book in the Bible – it was Jesus' hymn book – 150 songs, and so many of them tell us to make music and sing, rejoice through music, enjoy him through it. But Amos 5 places it all in context, telling us to make sure that our lives are also pleasing.

And so I've found myself scared to write songs about these things – I'm even scared to write this chapter. First because I'm no expert, and I certainly don't presume to be a teacher in these matters: I'm very much a learner, taking some baby steps in this area. But also because I don't want to sing or state bold claims about a matter so important to the heart of God and then fail to live up to those utterings. What I do know is that for so long we've been calling ourselves worship leaders, so perhaps it's time for us to explore some of the broader ways in which our lives can be used to lead worship for God.

COULD THIS BE ME?

There might be plenty of reasons that come to mind why we *don't* get personally involved with the fight against injustice and oppression, but there are just as many opportunities for us to be quiet revolutionaries wherever we look. We don't need a passport to make an impact. The tools are all around us.

Take eBay, for example. In the eBay generation we don't really dream of giving stuff away. We'd rather sell it. If we can get a few notes for something, we'll post it, wait for the bids and then pack it off. But how great would it be to trawl our houses for items that we can sell and then donate the proceeds to fighting poverty? How early Church is that?

My family is just in the process of moving house right now, and ringing in our ears are Jesus' words about how we should be giving away our excess possessions. After all, if we've got two of these items, do we really need a spare? It gets me thinking a lot these days, mainly about the notion that we hold on to everything we have because we believe that it is ours, not God's. We might like to think that our 10 percent tithe is our generous gift back to God, but are we really sure it was anything other than completely and utterly his in the first place? He's entrusted it to us, not the other way around.

The truth is that it is far easier to give our money, time and possessions away when we see them as God's, not ours. Put another way, one of the greatest obstacles to giving to the poor is the assumption that it's all ours in the first place.

But how do we know that it's the right thing to do? Perhaps it's because I'm stubborn and selfish, but I'm eternally grateful to God for the shocks that he's used to prompt me into action. Like the time when I found myself in a township in South Africa having just sold my house, waiting to buy another house. So all the money is sitting in my bank account, and I'm surrounded by poverty. God's message couldn't have been much clearer.

Then there was the time when, ten minutes after leaving a township, we drove past the holiday home of one of South Africa's wealthiest businessmen. Dripping with wealth, yet less than a couple of miles from unimaginable poverty – the taste in my mouth was foul. It came back to me when I was in Mumbai; just hours before, I had been drinking Coke by a pool in a Dubai hotel after a worship music event there – a place that, to those in the leper colony, I'm sure looked every bit as overblown and self-indulgent as Harry Oppenheimer's South African mansion. These shakes are vital. If we feel them fully they can point the way to a better, fuller, more radical life.

COMPASSION: MORE THAN JUST THE MONEY

There are some great child sponsorship ministries restoring hope to lives blighted by suffering. Some of them – particularly the more secular development agencies – suggest that actually meeting the person you're sponsoring would be off limits. The horror of a wealthy sponsor visiting an impoverished village sends shivers down spines.

But I don't think I agree. I think it takes away the distinction that the Church brings to all this. It says that all that matters in life is money – that all we can give is money. But is money all that we have to offer? Of course, giving our cash away is not an optional extra – no Christian's wallet should be closed – but nor is it the be-all and end-all of Christian sacrifice. The truth is, not only can we give more than just our cash, we can give of ourselves: our time, our energy, our sacrifice, our other resources. And not only can we give, but we can receive as well. Spending time with someone from another culture – while it may be a cliché – is often one of the quickest ways of learning something totally new about Jesus. Again, I'm no expert in these matters, but I do like to think that when it comes to the Church, a little face-to-face fellowship is always a meaningful part of the package.

I can still see the face of the guy with leprosy. I can see the face of the lady with AIDS in Africa. There's something about those images that will never fade. Like many, I've learned about joy in the face of suffering, generosity in the face of poverty, hope in the face of pain. It's the experiences we go through for ourselves that sculpt our land-scape far more dramatically than the theories we read about.

So the truth is simple: we need to get jolted, to allow our comfort-able bubbles to get pushed, squashed and popped by experiences beyond the typical. Why? Because isolation and exclusion do not look good on a follower of Christ.

It's up to us to act, time to get our heads around the verse that states, "From everyone who has been given much, much will be demanded" (Luke 12:48). With the privilege of feeling a sense of compassion rise within us, comes great responsibility to do something with it. My gut conviction is that putting that compassion to work might involve some grand things – perhaps a regular mission, raising money or raising awareness – but I think God wants to see it seeping into the details of our ordinary, unremarkable, busy lives. Perhaps it's as simple as thinking, every time we meet someone with less than us, about whether we should be giving them something. Perhaps it's tithing 10 percent of the money you made on your house sale, something we never earned but somehow didn't once think should be tithed to express our gratitude. Perhaps it means not letting the homeless go hungry or the lonely suffer in silence. Whatever it is for each of us, the formula will be flexible and designed to put the good news of Christ into living, breathing, tangible actions.

But what, you might be thinking, about all these problems? Surely they're too big to be overcome by us alone? It's true, there are times when we get paralyzed and overwhelmed by the sheer size of the problem – or freaked out by the inflated ideas about how we would have to behave in order to make a difference. We tell ourselves that it's an either/or situation: either we sell up everything we have and move to a slum, or we stay right where we are and concentrate on adding an extra zero to the end of our bank balance; either we leave our jobs and work for peanuts with a local charity or we ditch the idea of using all but the slimmest chunk of our time to help others. But it's not that way at all.

If all you believe you can do is get on a plane in order to reach poverty, then you need to get a better local map. If I tell myself that all I can do is hug a leper, then I need to take a closer look at my heart and my hands.

Perhaps this is the point about compassion: it is never the end point in itself, it is always the primer, the catalyst for change. In other words, just feeling it isn't enough; we must act on it. We sing our songs with good intent, but may our lives become the evidence.

POWER IN NUMBERS

While problems can be big, we forget the power that we have as members of the world's largest religion. We underestimate the power that we have as a united body. If everyone in the Church plays their part, then we can do massive things. We saw this recently at a large "Passion" event – a movement working with college students. Interestingly, students are a demographic group who are always being told that they are poor. But apparently if you're at college in America and are working part-time in Starbucks you're among the top 5 percent of the world's most wealthy individuals. So the chances are that you're not at all poor. The chances are that you've got incredible resources to make a real difference.

Louie Giglio and the rest of the Passion team tapped into this, pointing out that if we all give together we can achieve something. So at all the big Passion gatherings when you register you bring with you socks and towels for the homeless of the city. It's a pretty tiny sacrifice, and everyone can do it, but when that many towels and pairs of socks get donated free to those who can use them, you've just met a very real need in a city for a whole year.

There's another story from the Passion conferences, this one about Africa. These "poor" students ended up raising enough money to provide sixty African villages with water wells over the course of some recent regional events. Walking out of a meeting knowing that, because of this gathering, thousands of people will be given a better quality of life through the simple act of providing clean, safe water at the heart of a village – that makes you think. Sometimes you wonder whether all of our big gatherings are truly and utterly pleasing to God – and I hope and pray that they are – but under circumstances like those above you leave feeling a whole lot more assured that we really have brought honor and pleasure to the heart of God.

If we wake up to this mindset that we're better together, that these incredible resources are not ours but God's, then transformation of the communities we live near and far from cannot be far behind.

THE FUTURE IS LOCAL

We all know about globalization and the shrinking planet – how plans for faster planes, faster data and faster trade will make our boundaries and time zones even more obsolete as the years pass. But I'm not so sure that the best of the future is to be found here. I think the most exciting developments are going to come from local communities; I think that it's the local church that holds the potential for dealing with our most serious problems. After all, the local church has it all – the motivation, the time, the contacts, the drive to care for a person's complete needs. There shouldn't be one on earth that isn't caring for the oppressed, the downtrodden, the sick, the lonely. That's the way it has to be. And if there isn't something going on in your church, then start it.

Our big meetings will carry on happening and high-voltage anthems will continue to be sung, but wouldn't it be great if those crowds and that volume were a response to what was going on, not just a kick-start? Could it be that we're about to learn what it really means to live like the early Church? Could all that sharing and preaching and living and feeding and praying and changing that we see in Acts 2 be part of our nature as well?

THE MIDDLE OF
THE ROOM

Tim Hughes

The Spirit of the Lord God surely is upon us
Because he has anointed us
To preach the good news to the afflicted
We'll give out bread to the hungry
And open up our homes
And cover up their nakedness as if it were our own

And then our light will break forth as the morning sun
And the glory of the Lord will be our reward.
"Raise Up the Standard" by Kevin Prosch*

I USED TO JUMP UP AND DOWN TO THIS SONG. I'D BE THERE, IN THE MIDDLE OF THE ROOM, DOING THE CONGA. SOMETIMES I'D CRY, SOMETIMES I'D WEEP. SOMETIMES I'D GET SO EXCITED IT WOULD ALMOST BE AS IF NO ROOM COULD EVER BE BIG ENOUGH TO CONTAIN ALL THE PASSION I WAS FEELING. BUT AFTER THE 134TH TIME OF SINGING IT, SOMETHING HAPPENED. I SUDDENLY REALIZED THAT I WASN'T ACTUALLY DOING ANY OF THE THINGS THAT THE SONG TALKED ABOUT.

I wasn't giving my bread to the hungry. I wasn't opening up my home — or my parents' home — to the homeless. I wasn't covering up people's nakedness.

* Kevin Prosch © 1993 Liber Media & Publishing, llc/kingswaysongs.com

After so many times of singing about what I was going to do I finally had to face up to the fact that singing the song with passion just didn't seem quite enough. It left a large gap between my life and my songs, between the worship that I offered up in rooms full of Christians and the worship I failed to express when I was away from the crowds.

God's standards are high. And they are clear. We can't deny what the Bible teaches on issues of poverty and justice. When Jesus announced the start of his public work here on earth, he centered it on the impact his life would have on those whose lives have been scarred by injustice: 'The Spirit of the Lord is on me, because he has anointed me to preach good news to the poor.'

And if we're to be anything at all like Jesus, then his words must be our own.

I believe all of this. I believe that it's all true, that if the gospel means anything it will mean it to the poor, that it will break the chains of poverty and bring justice to the oppressed. But here's the thing that bothers me: how come there were so many of us back then jumping around in the middle of the room with empty words coming out of our mouths? How come the gap between what the Church should be doing and what we actually are doing has been so wide for so long? How come we got it so wrong?

Before we come on to wonder about some possible answers to this – as well as to kick around a few ideas about what life could be like if we did begin to narrow the gap further – it's time to think about fear.

There's a passage in the Bible that terrifies me. It's from Amos 5.

To the Israelite nation – who had trampled the poor, forcing them to give their grain; who had built for themselves vast mansions; who had abused and mistreated and taken advantage of those without the power to fight back – the Lord says,

I hate, I despise your religious feasts;
I cannot stand your assemblies.
Even though you bring me burnt offerings and grain offerings,
I will not accept them.
Though you bring choice fellowship offerings, I will have no regard
   for them.
Away with the noise of your songs!
I will not listen to the music of your harps.
But let justice roll on like a river,
righteousness like a never-failing stream!

Amos 5:21–24

Are our lives caught up in the same hypocrisy? Are we guilty of the same sins of greed and lies? Are we in the middle of the room with the ancients of Israel?

Take a look at the state of the world and the answer starts to emerge ... the United Nations estimates that unfair trade rules rob poor countries of $700 billion every year. This money that we prevent them from earning turbo-charges our own profitability, adding yet more luxury to our lifestyle, even more comfort to our air. Yet less than 0.01 percent of this money we skim from those with everything to lose could save the eyesight of thirty million people.

Or there's the fact that after a recent round of trade negotiations rich countries estimated that they would gain by $141.8 billion per year. Africa would be $2.6 billion per year worse off. The padding of our luxury grows with every abuse and betrayal we hand out to the very people Christ came to protect.

Have we developed a blind spot? Are we so comfortable in our lifestyle that we fail to notice the injustice all around us?

And what about me? I mean, if the Church – a body to which one in three people in the world belong – has not stopped such injustice, then what about my own life? Am I doing all that I can?

All too often we read these passages, we study them, and we listen to countless sermons and are challenged in the moment. We vow to live differently – meaning it completely sincerely – but the truth is that nothing changes.

It's as if we read these passages like Amos 5, and we rip them out of our Bible.

We read the words of Isaiah 10:1-2:

> Woe to those who make unjust laws,
> to those who issue oppressive decrees,
> to deprive the poor of their rights
> and withhold justice from the oppressed of my people,
> making widows their prey
> and robbing the fatherless.

We find excuses:

That doesn't apply to me.

Rip.

Or Matthew 19:16-22, when a rich young man approaches Jesus asking, "What good thing must I do to get eternal life?" Our mouths form around the words that Jesus offers in reply: "If you want to be perfect, go, sell your possessions and give to the poor, and you will have treasure in heaven."

Jesus can't actually mean that, can he? There must be some sensible, theological explanation.

Rip.

Or there's James 1:27: "Religion that God our Father accepts as pure and faultless is this: to look after orphans and widows in their distress and to keep oneself from being polluted by the world."

Are we called to really do that?

Rip.

And pretty soon we end up – as Jim Wallis says – with a Bible full of holes.

♥

Mark Twain got it right when he wrote this: "It's not the parts of the Bible I don't understand that scare me, but the parts I do understand."

We've been great at learning to understand God. We've done so well at bringing theology into the realms of the everyday that we all deserve a pat on the back.

But have we neutered our faith? Our theorizing and pondering and retreating into big halls for big conferences with big themes and little impact has threatened to leave our Church hollow and lifeless and lacking in integrity.

God's heart is clear; the songs we sing and the offerings we bring are totally meaningless unless they are offered out of a lifestyle of worship – a lifestyle that includes an active participation in caring for the poor.

We can't fool God. If we're not living the life, if we're not looking out for the last, the least and the lost, then it doesn't matter how amazing our songs are, or how fantastic the band sounds, or how emotional the night was – God's simply not interested.

I've messed up so often in this area. There have been times when I've been so consumed with the songs and the leading of worship that my first thoughts have always been about what's been going on right in the room: did people connect with it at all? Were they blessed? Were they impressed?

It never occurred to me to ask God whether he was into it or not.

The simple truth is that we have a tendency to become blind to the truth. We somehow miss the fact that issues of poverty, justice and money are all over the Bible. We forget that while idolatry is the most common theme in the Old Testament, poverty is the second. We look blankly at the fact that one out of every sixteen verses in the New Testament tackles the subject. In the first three Gospels poverty crops up every ten verses, while in the book of Luke it's there every seven. We read the Bible and somehow all this just passes us by. We're left doing the conga in the middle of the room, while the world aches outside.

★

Stop. This is only half the story. Something's been happening of late, and it's giving people hope. Today there are churches that are waking up to the importance of justice at the heart of Christian worship. Books capture the imagination; millions of Christians wear little white wristbands that unite politics and faith; action and activism stops being seen as a less valid form of worship.

I wonder if these days perhaps our actions are moving ahead faster than our songs. Hear me when I say this: we've not got justice sorted, not by a long way. Today – right now – there are still too many tears from too many people who are mourning the loss of a child, a mother, a father or a friend because some easily preventable disease claimed their life. But if we can get excited by issues of social justice, why do we struggle when it comes to putting the actions into words? Why is that? Why do we struggle to sing about it all?

Perhaps it is because our view of all this is too small. We see our songs of worship as vertical – simply going straight up to God – rather than connecting with those around us on a horizontal plane. It feels OK to sing about God's merciful heart for us, but it doesn't seem to inspire in quite the same way to sing about God's merciful heart for others. Perhaps it's because we don't like to be disturbed in our worship – because we like our times of singing to be inspirational, awe-inspiring and nicely intimate. Who wants to be thinking about God's love, his kindness and joy over us one moment, only to be ripped out of it the next to think about a girl sold into the sex trade ... it just doesn't compute. We think of God as being pure and wholesome and perhaps we don't want to spoil the moment.

It might feel out of sync with the way we've grown used to doing things, but take a look at the Bible and it's clear that there is plenty of horizontal sung worship going on; plenty of instances where God's people not only put God's hope into action but put it into words themselves – take a look back at the start of this chapter and you'll see one of the best known, taken from Isaiah 58.

Throughout scripture God is infinitely practical when it comes to giving his people instructions. He tells them how to farm, even dictating how the harvesters should not go to the very edges of the fields (Leviticus 19:9). That way, something is left for those who have no fields, so they can take the remaining produce to feed their families. And God asks the farmers not to go over the harvest twice, so that the fruit or grain left behind after the first picking can be used by others still without food. He instructs the vineyard owners not to pick up the grapes that have dropped off the vine (Leviticus 19:10) so the needy can pick them and their children can gain valuable vitamins and not be malnourished. These are laws based on mercy and kindness as well as an awareness of the importance of caring for others.

We see the same principles in Deuteronomy 15. Every seven years, debts are to be released for those struggling under the burden of owing too much to others (verses 1–2). It is clear that this is meant to be a new start. And God even makes the plans explicit by asking his people to interpret this rule generously and not refuse to lend to those in need as the seventh year approaches. Even if they know repayment is unlikely, they are not to show hard-heartedness or a begrudging attitude to someone who wants a loan (verses 7–10).

Can you imagine such an attitude in place today? The truth is that God is in the small print, he's not afraid of or removed from the detail. There are structures put in place and the people are to be held accountable for the way they implement them (verse 9). And all the provisions are put in place with one overriding aim in mind – that there will be no poor in the land. Yet while God talks about these plans in real detail, we struggle to sing about them. Couldn't our worship have a little more authenticity and challenge if we got some of these elements into our songs?

Perhaps there's another reason why we struggle to make our worship in song match up with our worship in action. Perhaps we've just never really worked out the link between the two. Perhaps we're still thinking that the two are removed and separate from each other. After all, we might be good at the songs of celebration, but have we really got a broad enough view of worship to be able to put all the psalms into modern-day worship sets? How would we cope with the songs of lament, the praise of creation and the fear of God's wrath? Maybe this narrow focus is just part of our nature, something we simply can't shift.

But something's changing. Songwriters now are starting to try to take their lead from those driving the Church forward, trying to be more of a minstrel than a muse. We're trying to find a more poetic way of talking about the topics that are defining the Church. We know that songs are important, that like other forms of liturgy they stick in the mind and are easy to remember, but more and more we are becoming aware of the gaps in our words. It's as if there's a ceiling with so many of our songs that limits how far we can really go with them.

Perhaps there's more to say about what we're *not* singing about. I'm often scared about really putting it all out there, scared of being totally honest about all the dirt and mess. I'm reminded of that famous prayer of St. Teresa of Avila: "O God, I don't love you, I don't even want to love you. But I want to want to love you." A lot of us are in that place but perhaps that's too personal and controversial to sing about. Perhaps this is one lament too far, too much reality for our services to cope with. What does that say about our worship? Is such honesty really OK for nuns from the sixteenth century but not for us today? Are we really comfortable wiping out the wealth and wisdom of history like that?

This gap that exists between what we sing and how we are starting to act might be an opportunity for us to think creatively in our worship, to start thinking outside the box. Perhaps this is the chance to look back and re-introduce ourselves to some of the elements of the service that we've thrown out. Could we link up music with prayers, a little like the old-school liturgy? Could we try and pray into a situation and then sing "Our God Reigns"? We could view some headlines in the news or startling statistics from the papers and follow it by singing "Lord, have mercy."

Enough of all these possible causes and reasons and reactions. The truth is that many of us have seen the difference that action has made to our sung worship. I don't know what comes first – whether the songs spark the social justice or the other way around – but I've glimpsed what it looks like when it happens.

It was back in 2004 that I first saw it in the flesh. It was an event in London called Soul in the City, and we had invited 10,000 young people to come to London and give up ten days of their summer for something bigger than themselves. They camped in fields, and we'd meet in the mornings to worship, pray and hear people talking about the way that God always sends us out – and then everyone would go into London, to work on the poorest estates and most neglected neighborhoods, doing simple, practical things like clearing rubbish, painting playgrounds or supporting local churches as they connected with their neighbors. It felt as though the intensity increased with every day that passed – the intimacy, the passion, the connection that people were making. It's not usually that way when you're leading worship for a bunch of young people who've only just crawled out of bed. It was the proximity of both these types of worship – through song and through action – that amped up the intensity of both. Suddenly the songs had way more power and the rubbish-clearing and painting was infused with way more purpose. The synergy between the two elements was electric and left thousands energized and inspired to pursue their faith with even more guts and passion and positive impact for those around them.

A couple of years later I saw it again, but this time smaller, in a community that bred intimacy and integrity in equal measure. It was David Ruis' church in Hollywood, and it managed to hold creativity in one hand and the ability to invite in the poor to be at the heart of the Church with the other. The unglamorous, real and raw downtown location helped add to the accessibility of the place, but it was about more than grungy walls and lo-fi coffee. Everything from the theology to the music to the honesty about people's brokenness seemed to fit. There was no pressure to behave in the right way or avoid offending others who knew more than you. Anyone could go in and be a part of the family.

One thing that struck me most about this church was the band. They weren't up at the front on a stage but in the middle, facing each other, just another part of the congregation. We've done this back at my home church now, and it really works. At times it's hard to tell where the band ends and the congregation begin. I think that God might like it that way. It seems to fit in with the idea of horizontal/vertical worship, as if by all being on the same level we have less baggage getting in the way of things being between us and God. As for the horizontal level, there's something incredibly powerful about looking each other in the eye when you're singing about taking your faith out to the poor and the broken. It's as if the whole church is making pacts and contacts with each other when they're singing these words, as if they create a stronger, more unified bond between each of the members of the church.

Perhaps putting the worship band in the middle of the room might be symbolically significant too. I wonder whether the time of the high-profile worship leader might be coming to an end. It's just a feeling, but I think it's possible that God's growing a generation of worship leaders and worshippers who belong fully in their community. Gathering together in large crowds has a potential and a power that we shouldn't lose, but they should never be at the expense of local action. So as things become more organic and local it might just be that small, often anonymous worshippers are finding their own songs to sing, without needing to climb on to a national stage.

When we drag our worship down from the stage and into the center of what we're doing – when we stop it just being about the five songs sung with perfect harmonies and start to sculpt it into something rooted in the lives and actions of the body of believers – then we're on to something that has the power to be honest and real. The church community I'm in is like any other – full of people with struggles and troubles, difficulties and hopes – and there's something about being surrounded by all this life that pushes me to want to find a way of bringing the angst and sorrows and making them worshipful.

All this leaves me wondering: what if we've created too many barriers and rules around our worship? What if one of the problems is that we've started to define it by what it isn't – worship isn't loud or provocative or for clubs or to be mixed with art or to be too showy or to be too quiet or to be too different? What if we reframed it all and started to look at worship in terms of what it *is*?

These prejudices piled up when I started visiting prisons. You don't ask a guy mixing your sound who happens to be serving a ninety-nine-year stretch in a maximum security Texan jail precisely what it was he was convicted of, but if you stop and think about it your imagination soon fills in the blanks. We were there to lead some worship with a crowd of male inmates, and it was clear that these guys were the ones that society just didn't know what to do with. They were the ones who had done great wrong to a great many people, the ones whose faces torment their victims in nightmares long after their trials are over – they're the scum of the earth. I don't say this lightly, but singing with them was probably one of the most amazing times of worship I had ever had.

To meet them and see their brokenness, to see that they're not so different from me, was humbling. Singing "Amazing Grace" and seeing so many of them weeping as they filed out, wearing their white suits, shuffling single-file out of the doors: surely worship has the power to break through our man-made boundaries?

Here's what I blogged about the experience when I got home:

I thought my heart would be hardened against them, I thought I'd despise them. But do you know what, my heart went out to them. They were warm, friendly, kind and encouraging. It blew our minds. In the midst of such evil we saw a light; we sensed something of God. Our sound guy – the one serving a 99-year sentence – was filled with the joy of Christ. Watching a number of these men passionately worship was one of the most incredible sights of my life. I will never forget one man weeping and throwing his hands in the air as we worshipped and sang about Jesus.

Here were a group of men who had sunk to the lowest depths. Living in a prison, with little to do. They're watched 24–7, treated with suspicion, deprived of any luxury; many serving time for mistakes made in their youth. Don't get me wrong, most of them deserved to be there, for the safety of society but also for justice's sake. But in this terrible environment, some of these men who had found faith in Christ clung to the hope and the truth that their sins had been washed away. Something truly great, a remarkable gift lavished upon them meant they could be made new – grace. It seemed fitting that they were all dressed in white, their daily uniform. A beautiful picture of what God's amazing mercy has the power to do.

> *Have mercy on me, O God,*
> *according to your unfailing love;*
> *according to your great compassion*

blot out my transgressions.
Wash away all my iniquity
and cleanse me from my sin . . .
wash me, and I shall be whiter than snow.

Psalm 51

I still don't quite know what to make of it all. To be honest I feel quite choked up about it. How amazing is our God that no one is ever discounted from his redeeming love? How incredible it is that God would have mercy on us, even though we've turned our backs on him time and again? How deep is his love that he would delight in a group of men whom the world despises? We've all fallen short of the glory of God, every one of us. We all stand as equal before him, but for those who've called him Lord, who have surrendered their all, for that person there is grace, hope, a second chance, and a new day.

♥

These barriers we've put up, they're not so sturdy after all. I've seen my fellow church members tear down the walls in a single night. They opened the doors to forty local homeless men and women, fed them, talked with them, manicured and pedicured them. They gave them mattresses and clean bed linen and invited them to sleep wherever they wanted in our newly carpeted church – new carpet that our vicar said had received the best ever christening we could have given it. With these men sleeping all over the church we were given a clear sign that if we want our worship to please God we need only follow the instructions already written out. If we want to put the poor at the heart of the church, sometimes we just have to literally get on with it and invite them in.

Our wealth can sometimes feel like a barrier – and it often is. We create lives of comfort and security that keep us insulated from the parts of life that scare us. Yet wealth doesn't have to be a barrier to working with poverty: shouldn't it make it easier? Anyway, I'm learning much more to worry a lot less about what others are doing with their money and to get to grips with what I'm doing with mine. There are a few people I could look at and say that I'm doing more than them, but a whole load more where I'm doing less. God calls us all to be obedient to his word – to care for the poor – and it's a responsibility that none of us can shake off. But we each need to prayerfully work out what it means practically for us. If I spend my whole time feeling guilty at not having moved to Calcutta, I ignore the opportunities that I have around me living in London – a city that's wealthy, but certainly full of need. Like the words that Micah gives in chapter 6 verse 8, we need to get active with our mercy – to love it, but not passively from the sidelines. The way we show that we love mercy should result in lives being transformed, and nothing less.

There are other barriers too. We can get duped into thinking that once we've done a certain amount of giving and sacrificial living, then we can flick the switch and forget about it. I might spend quite a lot of my time doing things around the issue of poverty and justice – and this CompassionArt project has been a great experience, particularly spending time with my mates writing songs – and in many ways it's easy to sign a check and send it off to a charity. Getting on a plane and visiting some projects in Tanzania isn't exactly hard work. But I'm kidding myself if I think that I've done enough. Are any of my friends in a position of need? How is my life really improving the lives of others who live near me? Is the world really the right way up with nothing left to fix? When I ask myself these questions I cringe with embarrassment – it's not at all like I want it to be. My life is not what I think it should be, and I get embarrassed at the number of times I get stirred and mentally commit to doing something yet never quite follow it through. I get caught up in the busyness of what I do, in friendships and family, yet too often I use this an excuse for what I *don't* do rather than letting God be the catalyst for what I *do* get around to doing. But if, as James Forbes said, "no-one gets into heaven without a personal letter of recommendation from the poor," my excuses really won't count for very much at all on the day that I'm called to account for the choices I've made in my life.

Many of us grew up with an idea that living the right way was a matter of avoiding certain sins. If we just kept ourselves within a certain spectrum of purity then all would be right with us, Now, while living a life that tries to avoid sin is a wholly good thing, it's not the only thing. Absence of bad stuff doesn't necessarily make for an abundance of good stuff. So it seems to me that the old compass that we've been using isn't working so well.

How come? Not messing up is no longer enough. We're into a gray area now, one marked by paradox. That paradox leaves us feeling unsettled and dissatisfied, wanting to do more – much more – with these gifts of wealth and time and space. And on the other hand there's God's continual grace – that he's pleased with us, that he delights in us, that he's proud of us. We could never live a selfless-enough life to warrant all that God has done for us, yet we know we must keep on trying. We could never be good enough, but giving up just isn't an option. You see it with King David, a man whose mistakes were colossal yet who could still write songs that are utterly soaked in God's love. "Keep me as the apple of your eye," he writes in Psalm 17:8, yet this was a man who cheated, lied and killed. If it were up to us, his lyrics would have stood a good chance of being wiped from public record. But God's not like us. When it comes to mercy, justice and humility he's not like us at all.

I can see a little of what David must have experienced in so many of my friends' lives. We get fired up about making a difference, we get excited about being forces for selfless good in the midst of all this selfish consumerism, and then we go and blow it. We spend too much, give too little, forget the good intentions or ignore the opportunities. We tell ourselves that this is the way it has always been, the way it will remain; we're selfish and greedy. We're singing empty songs while the world outside aches with poverty and preventable disease and premature death.

Then God's grace steps in. It breathes on us. It gives us hope and gives us strength. God takes our guilt – the guilt that makes us little more than glorified do-gooders – and puts something far more valuable and worthwhile in its place. He gives us forgiveness, mercy and the hope that we can do so much more with him in front of us than we could ever hope to achieve on our own. And then he sends us out again, tear-stained and weak-kneed, but back out to join the rest of the walking wounded, the ones who also need God's grace and mercy.

There's a myth that we in the wealthy West need something different from God than those who try to prize life out of a dollar a day.

It's just not true.

We all need the same kindness and love from God, regardless of how many keys we possess. We all need the same grace and tenderness, no matter how full our bellies. We all need God to help us fix the problems that surround us, no matter how low our resources.

The difference is only ever this: do we respond to God's challenge or do we ignore it? Do we worship with songs and deeds or do we not?

★

There's a clip on YouTube of Bono accepting an award. There are probably quite a few of them, in fact, but this one's special. Search it out – it's from the American National Association for the Advancement of Colored People and it was given in 2007.

His script is a few crumpled pages that seem to have some magnetic pull on his eyes. He tries for a few laughs, tries with the charm but gets dragged back to the pages in his hands.

And then something happens. He lets loose. He forgets the paper and the plan and speaks with more passion and guts than I think I've ever seen from him.

You need to watch it for yourself, but I'll just share this handful of jewels:

> True religion will not let us fall asleep in the comfort of our freedom ... Love thy neighbor is not a piece of advice, it's a command ... The poor are where God lives ... This is not a burden, this is an adventure ... Don't let anyone tell you that it cannot be done – we can be the generation that ends extreme poverty.

This is not a burden, this is an adventure ...

Our potential to change the world – with faith as our fuel – is not a burden. Our possibilities of finding a new set of songs to sing that embrace honesty and pain as well as challenge and truth – they're no more a burden any more than their arrival will be a sign of our individual success as songwriters or scribes. Our chance of harnessing the power of the Church's great numbers and using it to turn sorrow into dancing, oppression into freedom – living, breathing, sweating dances of freedom, hope and transformation – none of this is a burden. It is an adventure. A privilege. A birthright of every child of God.

So let's pause for a moment, right where we are in the middle of this room. Perhaps we don't have to leave the room after all. Instead, we can tear down the walls that keep our noise and joy and action separate from the world outside. Let's make this a bigger room, with a middle large enough for all.

THE JOURNEY BEGINS: Martin Smith with Jorani in Cambodia.

Stu Garrard, Michael W. Smith, Matt Redman and Martin Smith at the songwriters' retreat in Perthshire, Scotland, in January 2008.

Israel Houghton at Abbey Road Studios, London, February 2008.

Steven Curtis Chapman in Perthshire, Scotland, January 2008.

Les Moir, Martin Smith, Dan Needham, Michael W. Smith, Howard Francis, Israel Houghton, Stu Garrard, Tommy Simms and Danny Duncan (engineer).

Paul Baloche, Stu Garrard and Andy Park.

Tim Hughes and
Martin Smith.

Writing songs.

A big smile from Munny in Cambodia.

Paul Baloche, Israel Houghton, Martin Smith, Chris Tomlin and Graham Kendrick.

Anna and Martin Smith in Mumbai, India.

Martin Smith and Matt Redman.

Martin Smith, Mark Zschech, Matt Redman, Steven Curtis Chapman, Israel Houghton, Michael W. Smith, Tim Hughes and Andy Park.

Steven Curtis Chapman, Stu Garrard, Michael W. Smith and Matt Redman.

T ABBEY ROAD STUDIOS: Martin Smith, Michael W. Smith, Paul Baloche and Israel Houghton.

Chantou in Cambodia.

Martin, Anna and Ruby Smith visiting a Compassion project in Uganda.

Darlene Zschech, Graham Kendrick and Israel Houghton.

Michael W. Smith, Chris Tomlin and Israel Houghton.

Matt Redman, Stu Garrard, Graham Kendrick, Andy Park, Israel Houghton,
Tim Hughes, Jessica Park, Les Moir, Martin Smith and Paul Baloche.

Recording at Abbey Road studios – Stu Garrard and session musicians Tommy
Simms (bass), Dan Needham (drums), Akil Thompson (guitar)
and Howard Francis (keys).

Israel Houghton, Darlene Zschech, Michael W. Smith, Paul Smith and Martin Smith.

Michael W. Smith.

Graham Kendrick,
Andy Park, Darlene
Zschech and
Stu Garrard.

CompassionArt at Watoto in Suubi, Uganda, May 2008.

Aahlada in Mumbai, India.

Andy Park, Israel Houghton, Michael W. Smith, Graham Kendrick, Matt Redman, Darlene Zschech, Tim Hughes, Martin Smith, Steven Curtis Chapman, Stu Garrard and Paul Baloche.

A VISIBLE GOSPEL

Steven Curtis Chapman

SOMEONE ONCE ASKED ME HOW WINNING AWARDS COMPARED TO ADOPTING CHILDREN. IT WAS AN ODD QUESTION — NOT A BAD ONE, BUT JUST A LITTLE ODD. I MEAN, HOW CAN YOU REALLY LINE THE TWO UP NEXT TO EACH OTHER? I NEVER SET OUT TO GET AWARDS, EVEN THOUGH THEY'RE WONDERFUL SIDE-EFFECTS OF PEOPLE HAPPENING TO LIKE THE ART THAT YOU CREATE. BUT MY TOP GOALS HAVE BEEN HONORING GOD WITH MY LIFE, FINISHING THE RACE AS A HUSBAND AND AS A FATHER, AND HAVING MY KIDS KNOW THAT DAD LOVED THEM AND POINTED THEM TO JESUS. TO SEE OUR FAMILY GROW THROUGH THE MIRACLE OF ADOPTION FAR OVERSHADOWS ANY MUSICAL ACCOMPLISHMENTS, AND IT SEEMS TO ME THAT ADOPTION IS 100 PERCENT EVIDENCE THAT GOD IS AT WORK IN OUR FAMILY.

I would never have imagined seven or eight years ago that we'd have done this. I just thought our role was to be supportive of adoptive families. Yet God has done something amazing in putting us where he has at this point. It's not what I would call an accomplishment of ours — it has nothing to do with awards or the idea of someone telling you how well you've done — it's an accomplishment of God's.

But I'm going too fast here. I need to roll it back and start from the beginning, right?

It was my eldest daughter's fault. She started it.

Emily was eleven and was away on a mission trip with Mary Beth —

her mother and my wife – in Haiti. Now Emily had always been sensitive to kids who were troubled or in some kind of crisis, and so I suppose it wasn't surprising that she was stirred up by what she saw down there. But her reaction was really strong; she wanted to stay in Haiti to be with the children there. Mary Beth couldn't wait to get home to be able to eat something she could identify, but the only way of getting Emily home was with a heart on fire for conversations about adoption.

It wasn't going to happen. I was sure of that. There was no way that it was on our agenda. We had three of our own kids – two sons and a daughter – and busy lives. It simply was not an option.

Emily kept it up. She talked at us. She bought books on international adoption. She pestered us. She dropped facts into casual conversations. She left notes and letters for us. She got dirty, too, asking us to pray about it. She told us that if we wouldn't even consider it then there was a strong chance that we were "living in disobedience."

At first we were pretty good at resisting. We hit back with logical arguments. We laughed. We pretended not to hear. But then the cracks started to appear and we grew weak. We started playing the "what if?" game. What if we did adopt? What would life be like? Where would we adopt a child from? Whenever we played it we always had a picture in our minds of a child from Asia.

During one game we laughed a little harder than usual and decided that we ought to go and look up the Chinese character for "laughter" since the fact we were even considering it was completely hilarious.

A little later I was flipping through a stack of *Reader's Digest* magazines. I opened one at random and turned to a story about a family from China. It was interesting, considering our previous conversations, but it was when I got to the end of the piece that I stopped. Beneath the main picture was the caption:

The little boy's name is Shaohan (*Shao* in Chinese means laughter).

I showed it to Mary Beth.

She dropped the magazine.

And so our process of adopting from China had begun.

♥

About a year later, on 16 March 2000 we walked out of a hotel room in Changsha, Hunan province, China. In my arms was our second daughter, Shaohannah Hope Chapman.

Looking back on the journey, from Emily's persistence to the prayers of all our friends, God was all over it and there's only one word big enough to sum it up: miraculous. All the feelings and thoughts that you would expect to have were ours: could we ever love an adopted child the way we loved our biological children? Mary Beth was so afraid of adopting, but she knew that it was God who was calling us into this, so she took the little steps that she needed to, trusting God was in charge.

"I don't know what's going to happen to your mother," said Mary Beth to our kids when we went to meet Shaoey for the first time. But when Shaoey was placed in Mary Beth's arms, all those fears and doubts and worries were washed away. Mary Beth said: "God rolled back the curtain and said, 'This is your story, this is how I love you.' And he filled me with a love for her that I could never understand."

At that moment we knew that adoption was a very good thing that we'd be persuading others of in the future.

For us, though, this was a one-time deal. I was sure of that. Really sure.

After we started talking about how adoption had impacted our life, all these families approached us, saying they wanted to adopt but couldn't afford it. Mary Beth started writing checks and helping people, but a lot more families needed help.

We knew we had to get the Church involved and engaged in this, that this is what the Church is called to do. With all the financial resources we have in the Church in America, it's hard to believe that a child would ever go unadopted because of that reason. That seemed like something that people ought to set out to change.

What's more, we know that there are a lot of people who have room at their table but not room in their wallet for another family member. If God can adopt us into his family and call us his own, it is our hope that others might consider following his example by adopting a "father-less" child into their families.

So we started a charity that we called Shaohannah's Hope.* So far it has helped over 1,600 families to meet the cost of adoption. We help with both international and domestic adoption. We have a screening process and a committee of people who have experience with adoption agencies. You want to help as many families as you can in a significant way, so that it's not just a drop in the bucket. On our last tour, we raised funds for Shaohannah's Hope and used the analogy of building a bridge, because it's as if a child is on one side of an island and a family is building the bridge trying to get to them. They have all but ten feet of it built, but ten feet makes the bridge impassable.

---

* Shaohannah's Hope is registered as a legal nonprofit organization in the United States of America. The work of the ministry is best summarized by its tagline "mobilizing the body of Christ to care for orphans," with a specific emphasis on adoption assistance (financial grants), global awareness and orphan care (in-country care for those who remain, thus far specifically China and Africa).

Two years after we got back with Shaoey we were in a church at a dedication ceremony for the newly adopted daughter of some good friends. The Coley family had four biological children and five adopted children, and Dan, the father, is one of those prayer warriors who quietly gets on with the business of praying for certain people that they'd get the buzz about adoption. Apparently we'd been on his hit list for some time.

It was during that ceremony that I was sure God spoke to me about adopting again. It was as if he was saying, "This picture you are looking at is a picture of the gospel. It's messy and uncomfortable, and I know you have concerns and fears, but if you trust me with these things, I'm inviting you into this adventure again."

It's hard to turn that kind of invitation down. And probably not that wise either. So within a few days we'd started up again on the adoption process.

Bigger, wider things were going on at the time too. In 2002 I was captivated by the stories I'd been hearing of a handful of missionaries, and it made sense to include their stories when I went on tour. So during the second half of the show we'd tell people about guys like Nate Saint and Jim Elliot. They were killed by members of a very violent tribe they were evangelizing in Ecuador in 1956. Nate's and Jim's families continued the work they had begun, among the very same people who had killed these men, and their story is one of the amazing grace and power of the gospel. Mincaye, one of the natives from the jungle who took part in the killing of Nate and Jim, came out on tour, along with Steve Saint, Nate's son. Standing on stage with these two men — whose stories were bound up together through so much that was bad, but made whole by so much grace and love — showed me that compassion has a power greater than anything that could harm us.

During the summer that followed I took Will and Caleb, my two boys, on a trip to the Amazon jungle to visit the tribe. And yet again we found ourselves living a journey whose lessons would stay with us for ever.

It took a year for the adoption of our third daughter to go through, but eventually we heard that it was time for us to go and pick her up. There was a problem though: SARS was raging and Asia was literally closing down. But nothing keeps you from your children, right? So Mary Beth went out and brought Stevey Joy home to her family.

This was one of those turning points for me. I realized that none of this was about us doing our duty or our responsibility. It was not about us at all. Instead, it was all about God; how great is the love the Father has lavished on us, that we should be called the children of God? Isn't that what we are, adopted children of God? Didn't God come like a father and offer us the chance to know his love? I got the feeling that if we really did want to see God show up and make a difference in our lives, we needed to be open to God doing that in and through us, and adoption was the thing that we were burning about.

Through two adoption processes we'd started to get to know a little about China, and as the knowledge had grown so our heart for the place increased. I took more trips out to play there, and on one trip to perform at the Hard Rock Café in Beijing I ran into some missionaries. They had a baby with them, a little girl who, like so many, had been abandoned by her mother. They asked me if I wanted to hold her. I did. I asked them if they had adopted her themselves. They told me that they hadn't, that they were trying to find a home for her. I asked her name. They told me she was called Maria.

Immediately my mind started playing a song I had written years ago: "Who's Gonna Love Maria?" But it wasn't me singing it in my mind, but some guy with a big James Earl Jones voice. It was booming and shaking its way throughout every ounce of me.

A little later I called Mary Beth, in tears, and told her what had happened.

She told me: "Don't even think about it!"

But it was too late. I was already thinking about Maria and just couldn't get her out of my mind, although the situation wasn't as simple as the others. I didn't want to adopt again – I didn't feel we needed to – and Maria was a special needs child, already placed with an agency in a special needs program. Maybe we were just supposed to help her find a home.

I got back to Nashville. Mary Beth had the paperwork out already: "I think we're supposed to go and get Maria."

All the pieces fell into place amazingly quickly, and only a couple of months after I met Maria in Beijing I was back in China to pick up Maria Sue Chapman. She had a heart condition that classified her as "special needs," but to us it is clear that there are other reasons why she is special: she is ours. As the youngest of the family, she is certainly a handful, but Mary Beth and I know that our family would never have been complete without her.

★

Our family is now eight strong, and we believe our role in adopting children is complete. Then again, we've had those kinds of thoughts twice before. But what we do know is that we are meant to get involved with advocacy, which is why we started Shaohannah's Hope and why I'm using my chapter here in this book to talk about adoption.

I've been back to China a lot. In fact, as I'm reading this final draft of this chapter I'm sitting in a hotel room in Shenyang, China, having just arrived to do some concerts to raise money and awareness for the needs of orphans here. The government has been very kind and let me play on TV as part of a show that raises awareness about orphans throughout the country. I got to pay a visit to the Hope Foster Home (HFH), a place that provides care and surgical treatment for orphans who have surgically correctable defects. On other trips I regularly find myself performing for groups of orphan children or Christians. At one of these events I was playing and closed my eyes during the chorus of one song, singing, "Open the eyes of my heart, Lord, I want to see you." I felt God whispering to my heart: "Open your eyes, I'm right here in front of you." So I did. There in front of me was one of the orphans. He had crawled up and sat down in my guitar case. It left me in pieces on the floor as I felt Jesus saying, "Here I am, what now?"

So China has been good to us. It has given us three daughters and brought life into focus. We've grown in faith and taken risks that we would never have dreamed of years ago. And all because we've been able to take some small steps in our journey with God, just following on from one phase to the next.

It's not all China though. Mary Beth visited El Salvador in the summer of 2005, working on modifications to their child welfare placement system. It's the hope that adoption from El Salvador will become a whole lot easier in the future, and from her trip Mary Beth knows that the needs out there are great.

♥

In August of 2005, the whole Chapman family traveled to Uganda. We went up north, which is an area hacked apart by war and suffering.

Why? I guess we wanted to help if we could, as well as to learn about the war and how it has left so many victims in its wake.

We met some children at a local shelter in Kitgum. They call these kids "night commuters," but while the name sounds cute the reality is a long way from being pleasant. Each night, these young kids have to leave their parents and local villages and head to the shelter in Kitgum. It is there that they hide from the rebel terrorist forces called the LRA, the Lord's Resistance Army. The horrible truth about the LRA is that they have a campaign to take over the area by using its children. They raid the remote villages and kidnap the local kids. After that they brainwash them and train them to become killers. In just two years, over 12,000 children have been abducted and turned into LRA soldiers. Many of these victims shared their heartbreaking and horrifying stories of being forced to kill members of their own families — a brutal method of initiating the child soldiers and making it almost impossible for them to turn their backs on the LRA and return home.

The region is desperate for help. Orphanages need building, children need protecting and families need strengthening. It left all of us turned upside down, as Mary Beth explains:

We met a lady named Lois. She lives in a little place called Tender Trust and is caring for these precious children. There is no doubt that Jesus is there with those children and with the lady that loves them. You could tell Lois was in love, in love with the children, but even more so in love with her God. She was there out of a response to what Christ did for her.

By being there, offering herself as a living sacrifice, she is experiencing Christ's love, provision and protection in a very real way, in a way that most of us in our comfortable homes and safe neighborhoods will never know, unless ... unless we go, unless we do, unless we act.

Every day I am asking myself what this looks like for the Chapman family. I know that it is right that we choose to be deliberate and take our children on mission-type trips as well as to enter the baby world again by adopting our precious but very "high energy" daughters from China. Using our platform to make orphan-related causes known, and acting on solving them, makes sense as well, as we know that all this is on our agenda. But is this enough? Are we being cautious and holding back? Probably. I struggle. Is this enough? In simple obedience to the One who gave his life so that we might live eternally, we should desire to abandon all we know for the unknown of giving our lives away for him. It's not just about feeding the hungry, but entering into their hunger with them. It's not just about protecting them from a faraway safe place, but coming alongside them in their daily pain of being afraid. It's not just about appeasing our conscience by writing a check, but actually entering into their reality, a reality that needs to see Jesus. We should abandon all we know, but will we? God, help us to really hear you and to really obey.

★

It all started with Emily and a few days spent around poverty. The smells, the sights, the way that the stories captured her heart: this was all it took for the journey to begin. Years later we were hosting Chinese government officials from the Ministry of Civil Affairs and the director of the Chinese Center of Adoption Affairs in Washington, DC. We were able to distribute funds to support several government and private projects, including a government project assisting over 30,000 orphans in need of corrective surgery. None of this should make us proud — none of this is about us — but every experience and every child who gets medical care or every family that gets help with the $4,000 it costs in the USA to adopt from overseas, every one of these small steps is another stage on the journey with God. And it's a journey that has transformed our lives, and one it is a privilege to be on.

But it's bigger than what we first thought, bigger than us responding to the needs around us and helping a few people out. When it was time to write songs for a Christmas album all this became clear: we could be doing more.

The song "All I Want" arrived, the words falling out of me as I tried to describe a young orphaned boy who explains in desperation that his only wish for Christmas is a family. When it came time to take the songs on tour I knew I needed to step out into something a little bolder. Joining up with other organizations, it was time to bring on to the stage the American foster-care system – a system that does good things but that badly needs extra support. We managed to play to over 100,000 people and tell them a little more about the wonder of adoption. We also got to bring kids who were being fostered or who had been adopted on stage for the final song, "All I Want." It felt risky – it could easily be seen as a cheap way of getting the audience stirred up, a piece of exploitation of vulnerable kids. But we worked hard to make sure that they were not exploited or treated as objects, that instead this was an opportunity to make them feel special, significant and loved. Everyone worked hard to make sure that the children had the time of their lives.

So we managed to put the faces to the need, to make the facts come alive and allow people to make up their own minds about the potential benefits of adopting and fostering kids. Hundreds of people responded. Suddenly the presence of orphans was not just a matter of a big problem needing big solutions, but a series of individuals needing nothing more radical or complicated than a loving, caring family to welcome them in.

After this US tour we headed back to Asia to try and give something back to the region and the people who have given us so much. We ended up – all eight of us – spending a month working in Beijing orphanages. How was it? For each of us it was life-changing – yet again. And we can't wait to see where God will take us next.

♥

I have spent most of my life wrestling with the depth of scripture, baffled by its endless and eternal nature, confused as to how I am to grab hold of it with just the vapor of my life. But then we adopted Shaohannah. It was then that things started to make sense: without Christ to adopt and accept me I was hopeless, without a future, without a name … but then Jesus came into my life, gave me hope and a future. He gave me a new name.

Adoption is what John Piper calls the "visible gospel," a perfect picture of what God has done for each of us in making us his children through Christ. God's done amazing things in our family.

Hebrews 12:2 says, "Let us fix our eyes on Jesus, the author and perfecter of our faith." Without a doubt, adoption has been the most profound experience of my life, and my most profound experience of God. It has allowed me to understand what God has done for us, adopting us into his family, and it has given me the chance – time and time again – to look out and see Jesus as he locates himself among the poor.

The problems ahead of us are great. With an estimated 140 million children around the world living as orphans, and another child being orphaned every eighteen seconds, this is a challenge that we as a family and a charity are never going to fix. And I like that. It means that we are in way over our heads, that we are fully out of our comfort zones and that any success – any success at all – simply has to be thanks to God's grace and wisdom. We knew nothing about adoption when we started all this, and we're not experts now. All we are is hungry to follow God. There's nothing more to it than that.

So I suppose that's what I want to write about here in this book: the sense that when all's said and done, it's the following that counts. Obedience beats cleverness any day; saying "yes" to God is a far better strategy for life than telling him about our latest plans for greatness.

The visible gospel is not so exclusive – it is not reserved for people with money or access to the press or the time to fly off to China. None of that matters. What's true is that each of us has the option of putting our faith into action. We can each do something that pushes the boundaries of God's kingdom further, something that God leads, something that takes us out from our lives of isolation and comfort and out toward the places where our faith is needed most.

The visible gospel takes many forms. These pages have told you about the way that ours has taken shape, but yours may well be different. You may have seen it already – and if you're living it out right now you have my pride and prayers. But if you're yet to find your way on to the journey that God's laid out for you, then look and listen to the needs around you. They are everywhere, sometimes whispering, sometimes shouting, sometimes silent in a corner.

Will you go where they are calling you?

BAREFOOT ON THE MOUNTAIN

Paul Baloche

WE'VE DEVELOPED A BLIND SPOT. AND A DEAF SPOT. AND WRITER'S BLOCK. WE'VE HIT THE WALL, MISSED THE TURNING OR LOST THE MAP. TO BE HONEST, I'M NOT QUITE SURE *HOW* WE'VE GONE SO WRONG. ALL I KNOW FOR SURE IS THAT MANY OF US HAVE MADE SOME SERIOUS MISTAKES WHEN IT COMES TO LIVING LIFE THE WAY GOD INTENDED.

You want evidence? Well, where do we start? Do we take the fact that 30,000 children will die of preventable diseases by this time tomorrow? Or do we drag out the stat that one in three people on this planet – one third of our neighbors – live on less than a dollar a day, if you can call it living? Or do we look at the broken homes, the fractured communities, the blank eyes that stare three feet ahead as they hope for happiness and contentment in the latest, cleanest shopping malls?

Poverty – whether it's financial, personal or emotional – isn't a shame. It's a tragedy. And it's something we need to take personally – something we need to want to do something about.

It's taken the last couple of years for this realization to grow in me, but as the months have passed the sense that we – that *I* – have been missing the point has been taking shape. And lately, that shape has become clearer. As I've been thinking and praying and wondering and reading and asking about it all, I think I've got a better clue of how we managed to get into this state.

And it's all found in the ancient scriptures. I'm convinced that it's because there are places in the Bible that have been overlooked, places that have been undersung. And Micah 6 is one of them.

> With what shall I come before the LORD
> and bow down before the exalted God?
> Shall I come before him with burnt offerings,
> with calves a year old?
> Will the LORD be pleased with thousands of rams,
> with ten thousand rivers of oil?
> Shall I offer my firstborn for my transgression,
> the fruit of my body for the sin of my soul?
> He has showed you, O man, what is good.
> And what does the LORD require of you?
> To act justly and to love mercy
> and to walk humbly with your God.
>
> Micah 6:6–8

Why isn't this at the top of the list of Things That We Sing About? Why aren't those last three lines the basis of all our actions? Why isn't this etched into the glass over every mirror we own? If for some reason we lost all the pages of the Bible — if all those stories and instructions were lost forever — all apart from this one passage, don't you think we'd still have a chance of living a life that pleased God? Just think about it for a while — isn't it all there in those twenty-two words — everything we need to know about how our faith ought to be acted out?

The King James version puts it beautifully too, making it clear that every cell and fiber and thought and action ought to be channeled to "do justly . . ." as well as love mercy and walk humbly. It makes it seem so easy – just "do" justly. Yet we make it all so complicated. I love the simplicity of it all – the idea that by treating people with justice, treating them with fairness, treating them with kindness, we in some way find ourselves on the path that pleases God.

It's all so practical that it's impossible to read the passage without thinking about how it ought to – or just how it might – make an impact on our lives. I mean, just think about it: if being merciful became something that we loved, something that we really couldn't get through the day without, then how would that impact the world around us? How would the micro and the macro, the individual interactions face to face and the parts we play as global citizens – how would they be impacted? If we did the same with justice – pursuing what is right and fair with all our strength in every action – couldn't the world look a little better than it does right now?

There's a key to all this, and I think it's found in the last part of the pie. It's the idea of walking humbly with God that holds the key to it all. It's easier to be merciful and easier to extend grace in our marriages, toward our children, our neighbors, when we're aware of our proper place in the great scheme of things. Or, to put it another way; when life becomes all about us being the directors, stars and scriptwriters – when today becomes a platform for performance in our own strength and by our own guidance – then being compassionate, kind, merciful and self-sacrificial gets a whole lot harder. Ask any of the people I work with: when I'm setting the standards and feeling ambitious then I'm not the nicest guy to be around. I hustle and hassle people as humility goes out of the window.

★

Before we look at ways that all this can get put into practice, it's worth pausing and asking precisely what we don't mean by humility – what isn't it?

It can feel as if humility is that wallflower guy, the one with sand falling from his face, the total wimp who has never had any ability to stand up for himself. Scratch beneath the surface and a lot of us have an idea that Jesus is a little bit like this too. He flits around our minds, a guy in a robe, all meek and mild, certainly underwhelming with his passion – not the kind of guy to break into a room and start shouting and screaming. We like our Jesus to glide, to calm the storm with a whisper not a roar and a rant and a rage.

Of course, when you see it in black and white it all looks kind of ridiculous. We know that Jesus wasn't afraid of ruffling feathers and kicking over tables, but still this idea of trying to follow him in his humility leaves us pulling the plug on passion and fight.

Whatever this virtue called humility is, Jesus was obviously the very best living example of it that the world has ever seen. As the living incarnation of God, there can't ever have been a better example of humility around, right? He must have been the embodiment of it. Yet at times he was raging among the crooks and the crowds of cowards, turning those tables over. He's the one who said, "Before Abraham was, I AM." He's the one who went to *that* death. If humility is about having a diminished sense of self-worth, you don't walk into a death like that with such dignity and trust.

So walking humbly probably looks a little different from the ideas that might first spring to mind. I'm convinced that it brings with it many other things – a sense of gratitude, for example, and a sense that we don't have to earn our place. Surely it helps us to realize that God has said to us, "You are my child; I am for you, not against you. I love you, I want to see you grow up to become molded into the image of my Son." Having thoughts like this at the core of your being lights the way to a better future. God is on our side and he loves us, not for what we can do for him but simply because that's the very nature of who and what he is — that he offers love and grace to all. If we can really believe it and let it guide our steps, then who knows how much better the world could look?

♥

This whole idea about walking humbly with God . . . it's got me thinking. It's almost as if you want to turn that scripture backward — to make it read that, as we walk humbly with the Lord, it's as if our heart is brought into line. In turn that gives us compassion and mercy toward others when we see them messing up. Instead of jumping on them, we're in a state of submission to the Lord, a state where we're aware of our shortcomings and failures. And it drives us toward fighting for justice for others, since the greater the awareness we have of what God has done for us, the more hungry we are that others are able to live their lives free from oppression and injustice and better able to soak up more of the good things that God intends for all.

Rosa Parks. Martin Luther King. Gandhi. How's that for a list of people who understood the incredible power between a humble walk and a revolutionary life?

The US Congress called her "the mother of the modern-day Civil Rights movement," but Rosa Parks just knew her place. She knew that leaving her seat so that a white gentleman could take it would be a mistake. As she later said,

When that white driver stepped back toward us, when he waved his hand and ordered us up and out of our seats, I felt a determination cover my body like a quilt on a winter night.

People always say that I didn't give up my seat because I was tired, but that isn't true. I was not tired physically, or no more tired than I usually was at the end of a working day. I was not old, although some people have an image of me as being old then. I was forty-two. No, the only tired I was, was tired of giving in.*

Rosa Parks walked humbly with God and she knew her place — and it was not as a second-class citizen. It might seem strange to say it, but on that bus, at that time, humility did not mean giving in. Humility for Rosa Parks — and the millions who would benefit from the emerging Civil Rights movement over the following years — looked like standing up to injustice.

Martin Luther King's determination to find nonviolent forms of protest speaks of a dependency on the Lord and hints at the roots of the incredible authority that covered his words. He was prepared to walk humbly, to endure taunts and abuses and even the ultimate sacrifice, the highest price. Yet when he was attacked, Martin Luther King did not pay back evil for evil. He didn't attack police stations or start riots, and he refused to make the movement about his own personal gain. Of course he wasn't perfect — none of us are — but his life remains an example of the way that God can use those who are willing to put themselves in the firing line because of what they believe. It takes a certain type of humility to do that — a knowledge that God can be trusted and followed even though the fears crowd around on both sides.

* Rosa Parks with Jim Haskins, *Rosa Parks: My Story* (Scholastic, 1992).

The idea of celebrating a man like Gandhi in a book like this may be offensive to some Christians – but to me his life is another example of humility with flesh on the bones. He's inspiring – the way that again he pursued justice through nonviolence, the way that he lived, makes me sure that he was trying to follow Jesus, to behave like him. I don't feel like I do it enough.

These examples of humility, mercy and justice changed the world. Thinking about them makes me confident that this is enough, that Micah 6:8 really can be trusted as a compass for our lives. So much of the New Testament is caught up in the idea that there is a "finished work," that the greatest accomplishment of God is already done; the writer to the Hebrews adds to it by making it clear that we're here to add praise rather than create salvation for ourselves. So what else other than humility, mercy and justice do we really need?

★

It's all well and good knowing that we ought to know our place with God – a place from which we will speak out, stand up and lay down our agendas – but there's an important question that I'm confused by: why is it that we have overlooked this for so long?

I'm like a lot of people who have been saved out of the alcohol and drugs scene. God radically turned my life upside down – or I guess I should say right side up – but sometimes it has been hard to leave the old patterns behind. That hunger for something new and exciting, the next hit that shakes your world and leaves you convinced that finally you've cracked the code . . . it's hard to leave those patterns behind. They might work OK in a club, but the attitude just doesn't come out at all well in church. We get tempted to treat this new teaching track or style of worship or spiritual tangent as the thing that we ought to drop everything for, ignoring the essential truths that have been in place for years.

Why do we have such a hunger for the next big thing? Has it always been this way, ever since the days of forbidden fruit and people grumbling in the desert? Perhaps it's just a part of our nature. But while I know that a lot of us who have been Christians for any length of time fall into the trap of waiting for whatever it is that's next on the horizon, it still doesn't seem quite right.

And perhaps it isn't. Perhaps it is this passion for the next book, the next teaching, the next big thing, that lies behind our mistakes. Perhaps we need to stop for a minute and absorb the truth that is all around us – that God has already shown us what is required, he has shown us what is good, and that if we just spent our lives working on that then we'd find ourselves in a far better place.

And then again, maybe we find ourselves getting sidetracked away from the basic, often dull questions of how our lives are matching up because it all just seems too basic. Walking humbly? How can that ever sound exciting? What about loving mercy – isn't that just a little bit too much like Sunday school? And as for acting justly: aren't there better things we could be doing with our time – like preaching, evangelizing or leading the way to the moral high ground?

It's almost as if it's some kind of offense to our minds to believe that the path to us transforming the world lies, as Christians, in something as simple as dealing with our attitude. If doing well means being less impressive, are we really ready to join in?

"Knowledge puffs up, but love builds up" (1 Corinthians 8:1).

He's right. We may not like it but our tendency is to formulate great ideas and add more words and sell more books and make more of anything else that we can find. Why? Because we can't really deal with the fact that this idea of a practically surrendered life is what God's after. It might be revolutionary, but the idea of waking up in the morning and deciding to give the hours that will follow over to God and others just doesn't seem all that attractive.

♥

As well as the grand stuff – the bold moves of Rosa Parks, Dr. King and Gandhi that have changed the world – there are smaller, quieter symptoms of a humble walk with God. OK, so the idea of walking anywhere these days seems a little odd – let alone doing it humbly. But when we see that this journey we're on is one with a destination and a purpose – justice and mercy – and a partner – the Lord God himself – then it starts to take on a whole new feel.

If we start our days in humility, being thankful to God for what is around and in front of us, being open to following his plan, then life is simply better. If we can start off by admitting that "I can't do this in myself, I can't live the Christian life by myself, in my own strength" and that we need God to be the guide to lead us ahead in our steps, then again we find ourselves on a far better path.

And in the paradox of God's grace something strange happens. When we decide to let God be in charge we find that ideas of improving our own reputation or securing our own advantage seem to have less of a hold on us. We end up feeling energized and a little more full of life when we walk humbly with God. That grace then starts to flow out to others as we go a little easier on them and act a little more kindly. We end up as better listeners and kinder, more caring parents, partners and friends. We just get better at being better.

★

One last point. The Bible doesn't just say that we should *sit* humbly; instead it tells us to *do* something. As in the parable of the talents, where the man who chose to do nothing with his investment received criticism; God is not a god of inactivity. We are made to be involved, to act as salt and change what we rub up against. Humility involves actions, and little ones too. There's nothing quite as ordinary as walking, but that's the link that Micah 6 makes: that our very steps – and we take thousands during our days – should be branded by a humble dependence on God. It doesn't just say that we should sit in a lotus position and contemplate the notion of perhaps becoming one with humility. We are told to walk – and live – it out.

So the practical art of living this way gets spotted by those in the know. Take a look around you and you might be able to see the signs of those who have grasped hold of Micah's call. They'll be the ones who are the better listeners, the ones who are flexible when the situation demands it, the sort who are undeniably used by God but who would be the last to use that fact as a boost for their own status. They're the ones who are moving on in their lives, who are changing their neighborhoods and communities for the better. They're the ones who stand up for the weak and the downtrodden, who do not hold on for revenge, but who are able to admit their faults and not press others to do the same. They're full of grace and passion, determination and inspiration. At times they're ordinary people living ordinary lives; it's their attitude that defines them, not their bank balance, job titles or post codes.

They're the ones who are transforming this world for the glory of God.

FRIENDS OF
THE POOR

Andy Park

TRANSFORMED

I was just another teenager living through just another first year of university, but my life was being transformed. I was living through a revolution, one that left me on a totally different course from the one I'd been on before.

It was God who was doing it. Powerful encounters with him, especially through worship music, were the primer that introduced me to the power of the Holy Spirit and the reality of God's life-changing love.

I watched people around me during my first worship service in a Vineyard church. It was an other-worldly experience; as people were pouring out simple love songs to God, giving and receiving love, a whole new world opened up to me. I began to know God, to hear him speaking. And almost immediately I began to write songs.

I had never written songs before, but now they were gushing out of me. In the years to come I would find myself receiving and writing hundreds of songs, all flowing through me because of the simple fact that God had captured my heart. He revealed himself and I couldn't stop writing about it. I hadn't planned or hoped for it; it was spontaneous combustion.

But it wasn't all about soaking it up. Somehow, I had to give it away. This river of God's blessing that was pouring into me obviously wasn't meant just for my own benefit. I wanted to let it flow outward. I wanted to give something away.

Why? Because as a church we simply have to follow Jesus' example of generosity and compassion.

PROPELLED

In worship, God's truth presses in on us and propels us outward. For the worshipper there's a never-ending cycle of absorbing more of the love of God and a corresponding urge to spread that love around. This vision has shaped my ministry job description. Though my strongest area of ministry is music, I've never given all of my time to music. Music ministry and mercy ministry have an interdependent and synergistic relationship. If I worship and see Jesus, I must show mercy to the poor — and if I spend myself on behalf of the broken, I feel a need to worship and be filled up with God's strength once again. The two are meant to live and breathe together.

It's not all that surprising, really. The two greatest commandments of Jesus are very closely intertwined — love God and love your neighbor. You can't love God with all your heart (and sing lots of songs to him) unless you also love your neighbor as yourself. If we only show our love for God by singing, God is not the least bit interested in listening. Several of the prophets had a lot to say about the corrosive side-effects when the singing and celebrating were combined with a lack of justice, and it only takes a quick look at Amos 5:21–24 to see how seriously God takes it all.

Worship is about joining his cause; giving his love to others. We sing "give me your heart, Lord," "make me more like you, Jesus." What is Jesus like? What is his heart like? It's full of compassion for other people, especially the poor. The very first thing Jesus said when he publicly announced his ministry was that he was coming to the poor:

> The Spirit of the Lord is on me,
> for he has anointed me
> to preach good news to the poor.
> He has sent me to proclaim freedom for the prisoners ...
> to release the oppressed.
>
> Luke 4:18

We love it when the Spirit "comes upon us." I really love it. But God doesn't anoint just for our own benefit. The river comes in and the river must go out.

When we see Jesus, we see the great giver. We see that it truly is more blessed to give than receive. We're so grateful when we ponder the mercy of God lavished on us – our natural response is: "How can I show my gratitude?" "In view of God's mercy" (Romans 12:1) we give our bodies – not just our meditations, but our energy and time – to making a difference in our world. Through simple acts of kindness and joyful sacrifice, we proclaim the worthiness of Jesus by emulating his life, allowing God's love to propel us in the direction his Son took: outward.

Mark Labberton has written a book on the life-changing implications of worship for every Christian. He opens our eyes to a rich biblical look at what worship really is:

> Worship here refers to what matters most: the way human beings are created to reflect God's glory by embodying God's character in lives that

seek righteousness and do justice. Such comprehensive worship redefines all we call ordinary. Worship turns out to be the dangerous act of waking up to God and to the purposes of God in the world, and then living lives that actually show it.*

In his book *Let the Nations Be Glad*, John Piper describes worship as both the fuel and the goal of missions:

> When the flame of worship burns with the heat of God's true worth, the light of missions will shine to the most remote people on earth. Where passion is weak, zeal for missions will be weak.

Piper goes on to say that:

> the goal of missions is the gladness of the peoples in the greatness of God . . . Worship is the goal of missions because in missions we simply aim to bring the nations into the white-hot enjoyment of God's glory.†

ACTIVE

Getting transformed and then propelled outwards is an inevitable consequence of truly experiencing the great love of God; we get changed into worshippers and mercy-givers. When we see the glory, power and love of God as revealed in Jesus Christ, the natural and necessary response is extreme worship and generous mercy.

* Mark Labberton, *The Dangerous Act of Worship: Living God's Call to Justice* (IVP, 2007).
† John Piper, *Let the Nations Be Glad: The Supremacy of God in Missions* (second edition, Baker Academic, 2003).

When we discover God through worship, he calls us to follow in his footsteps. When we become wed to Christ, we are wed to his cause. When this happens we get active.

Over and over again in scripture we see a progression of revelation, worship, transformation and action. There's no such thing as worshippers who have zeal for God but no love for their neighbor. Instead, there's a roll call of well-known biblical worshippers who were outstanding in their service to others:

God reveals himself to Abram, and sends him on a harrowing journey of faith into a foreign land. Abram's sojourn arises out of worship and revelation, but has a purpose far greater than his own life and family. All along the way, God promises to bless Abram and to make him a "blessing to all nations." Blessing others was integral to the experience of knowing God.

Isaiah was entranced by a vision of the Lord in the temple, complete with worshipping angels, an outpouring of smoke and the shaking of the building. He was cut to the heart by an overpowering vision of God's holiness. When he cries, "Woe is me, I am a sinful man," an angel comes to touch his lips with a coal from God's altar, symbolizing cleansing. Immediately, Isaiah is recruited by God to go and spread God's message. True worship turns us inside out. We get cleaned up on the inside, and we give out the mercy we've received.

The New Testament tells the same story. When the disciples caught a glimpse of Jesus – his authority, his love and his miracles – there was no choice but to follow him. For them, worshipping the Messiah meant a total change of occupation. They saw that Jesus was worthy of their utmost loyalty and devotion. When he said, "Come, leave your nets, follow me, I'll make you fishers of men," they left immediately. Their lives were turned upside down.

Saul of Tarsus, an ardent persecutor of the fledgling movement of Jesus people, was traveling to Damascus one day when he was arrested by a revelation of Jesus. He saw a flash of light, was blinded, and then his spiritual eyes were opened to the reality of Jesus the Messiah. Saul became a new man with a new name and a new goal in life. Soon after his first encounter with Jesus, Paul was on his way, commissioned as the "apostle to the Gentiles." For Paul, revelation gave birth to worship and mission.

REAL-LIFE EXAMPLES . . . INDIA

It's not all ancient history. It's happening right now too, in communities and neighborhoods the world over.

I went to Chennai in India and saw it for myself. There is a church out there that is doing incredible things for the downtrodden and oppressed. They've got an incredible bunch of talented musicians among them, but their artistry and love for worshipping God doesn't stand alone — it is matched by a commitment to mercy ministry.

John Christian leads the church and their Acts of Mercy outreach. He took me on a tour of the school building they have reclaimed and refurbished in a rural area about an hour from Chennai. Previously this building was a brothel — a brothel of the worst kind, a dark, filthy place soaked in abuse and oppression. But Acts of Mercy have transformed it into a beautiful school they called the Achievers' Academy. These days they reserve half of the places in the school for the poorest of the poor, and the results are profound; and all of this was done by faith, one step at a time. God's compassion compelled John and his team to attempt the impossible, and God came through with the provision to secure the building and nurture these dear young children.

The realities of life in India are harsh: if you are stuck at the lowest socio-economic strata, you are ostracized and rejected; you can't get out of poverty by yourself. Acts of Mercy empowers people to climb out of that pit of hopelessness. It teaches them to read and write and sets them up with skills that will enable them to get a job and start to build for themselves a far brighter future.

Many of these kids are fatherless — their fathers have either died or abandoned the family. When left alone, the mothers suffer in many ways. Through the oppressive social systems of their community and village leaders, these women are forced into lives of debt, dependency and obligation. Some of them fall into prostitution in a desperate attempt to survive. Acts of Mercy is helping raise these women out of oppression and despair.

There's another element to their work: job training for single mothers to help them become independent and able to provide for their families. I met several of these young ladies who were being trained to be tailors, and they were some of the most radiant and humble people I had ever met — shining with gratitude and joy. No longer will they live marginalized lives. No longer will they be ashamed and trampled by the oppressive ways of their culture. No longer will their life be clouded by sorrow and fear. They are gaining skills that will help them find jobs and even start businesses of their own; new hope grows within them.

There's even more to the church too, since they've just started building apartment blocks for widows and providing all kinds of life-skills training, as well as developing a poultry and bovine farm.

It's all so much like Psalm 113. In this ancient song of worship the writer says that God

raises the poor from the dust
and lifts the needy from the ash heap;
he seats them with princes,
with the princes of their people.
He settles the barren woman in her home
as a happy mother of children.

Psalm 113:7-8

This ancient liturgy from Israel's worshippers is exactly what I saw happening through the work of Acts of Mercy.

As the people of the church sing about the Father's love, they also live it out. In countless simple, practical ways they're putting into flesh and blood the words of their songs, giving these dear people a place to belong, a hope for a better future and a living touch of God. They are an incarnation of the Lord's love; they are being fathers and mothers to the fatherless.

REAL-LIFE EXAMPLES . . . CANADA

It was back in 2006 that we started a new church plant in the red light district of Surrey, British Columbia. The neighborhood is full of addicts, sex trade workers and homeless people, and our little church exists to befriend and help these folks.

It's not a swift process, but slowly and surely the folks in our church are befriending some of the needy of our community – including refugees from Africa and Thailand, and recovering drug and alcohol addicts from Vancouver. We're learning how to help addicts transition into normal lives and to support refugees as they try to assimilate and survive in a brand new culture.

For those of us involved in it all, this church plant is a new stage of our voyage that is taking us through uncharted waters; it requires us to continue learning and depending on Jesus to do things we can't do on our own. Our worship life must keep thriving if we are to have the wisdom and inspiration to keep going and giving.

It's the fact of making connections with people — of putting ourselves in positions where we will meet, get to know and grow with those who have far less than we do.

Through some Catholic friends of ours we found out about a group of refugees in our city called the Karin people. The Karin are Christians from Myanmar who were persecuted by radical Muslims and fled across the border into Thailand, where they settled in refugee camps. A handful of our families have befriended Karin families and have helped them with groceries, in applying for jobs and accessing various government agencies. Because they come from the jungle, they know nothing about the complexities of living in a Western culture. They need friends to show them the way and help with the language barrier.

Nowai is a single mother of five children. During a war in Liberia, Nowai's husband was killed, and she fled with four of her children to Ghana, where they landed in a refugee camp for eleven years. Then the United Nations relocated her to Surrey, B.C. Two of our couples met her one day when our church was doing a free barbeque in the low-income apartment complex where she lived. At that time, she couldn't walk because of excruciating back pain. Our people prayed for her and she was healed on the spot. In the ensuing months, our church provided lots of groceries, furniture for their flat, help with accessing government aid, and friendship. Again, people took the initiative and made time to offer practical help.

A couple in our church named Greg and Rebekka feel drawn specifically to foreigners. Greg explains:

When we were working in North Africa we were in a city in the middle of the Sahara Desert where there were no other foreigners. As a result of being alone there we were forced to seek friendship from people around us; people from other religions and cultures. We were so warmly welcomed by people even though we were the "western enemy that people were taught to hate and fear." All we had to do was walk along the street and people would invite us into their home for a meal.

Back in Canada, our eyes were opened to how unwelcoming we are to people from other cultures. We rarely make the effort to reach out in friendship to them. We've tried to see people as friends — as people and not just projects.

Rebekka tells of one such friend:

There's a Muslim woman I met at Willow Glen [a low-income apartment complex we visited monthly for the first year of our church plant]. She told me about a dream she had about Jesus. I'm amazed; she still has dreams from God; God is speaking to her. Spiritual things are happening in her life. I wasn't pursuing spiritual things, but she keeps bringing it up.

People really open up when you're friends with them — they will ask for prayer just because you're friends with them.

Regarding Muslims, Rebekka says: "It's not their custom to pray for each other, but once you offer to pray for them, they'll take the initiative to ask again in the future."

Greg and Rebekka have found that getting to know people as friends actually increases your compassion because you're learning things about them. You find out so much more about what people are going through.

Rebekka told me: "I'm kind of in shock about the hard things people go through." She has heard lots of stories of husband–wife abuse, extreme poverty, and lots of death.

Recently one of the families from this same apartment complex phoned Greg and Rebekka when they found out that the wife's brother had been shot in a drug- and gang-related incident. This particular family is from the Sudan, in Africa, and they speak limited English. Greg and Rebekka offered to help them in any way they could. Going with this Sudanese couple was quite an experience, says Rebekka: "It was hard to see them grieving their brother." Because Greg and Rebekka have visited this family many times, given them rides to church and even cared for their kids during church, the Sudanese couple naturally called them for help.

Greg shared insightfully from this experience: "You don't need any special language abilities or special funding to help people. It's mostly just giving them time, patience and understanding. It's about taking the time to contact the right agencies and people."

We spend so much of our time thinking that our "stuff" is what counts, that it's our possessions that we ought to be giving away. But for most others the most valuable thing we can give is ourselves – our time, honesty and energy that allows us to form relationships with others.

HOME

Simple friendship is our main way of helping people who are broken. And when it happens in our own home the results can be even greater. One day, a teenage girl I'll call Debbie was at our house for dinner. Debbie was coming out of drug and alcohol addiction, and her home life was a wreck – her mother had been with three different men, and none of them had cared for Debbie with real fatherly compassion.

When Debbie saw me tickling one of my young sons and laughing and wrestling with him, she said, "Wow, I didn't know fathers ever treated their kids like this." It was like a revelation to her – something completely foreign to her own family of origin. Her own father did a lot more yelling at her than anything else.

Time after time I've seen a profound visitation of the Holy Spirit when worshipping with needy people. In a poor community in the Philippines where people built shanties over the top of a cemetery, the Spirit came in power. In a noon-time Bible study for a small group of addicts in Surrey, the Spirit came in power. In Saturday night worship times attended by homeless people in Surrey, the Spirit comes in power.

One of the most powerful outpourings I've ever seen of God's love and healing during worship was in an outdoor worship festival in Mongolia. Even with a language barrier, many of these poor rural people received healing with tears as the ministry team prayed for them and the music washed over their souls. God is the "high and lofty one" who also dwells with those who are lowly and contrite – with those who know how much they need him.

RISKS

Of all the uniting threads that pull together these stories of worshippers who touch the poor, one common thing is that they push outside their personal comfort zones to do the uncomfortable act of bringing comfort to others.

When the white-hot revelation of the glory of God bursts in, worshippers do things that aren't normal. They march to the beat of a different drum. The Bible is full of people who were captured by a revelation from God and then stepped outside their comfortable routine.

As a worshipping teenager, David's zeal for the Lord energized him to risk his life to defend the Lord's honor. His heart of worship drove him to attempt the impossible. David rejected the armor of Saul and plunged into battle, trusting in God's authority rather than the inventions of men, rejecting them all: "sword and spear and javelin." He challenges and slays the giant so that "the whole world will know that there is a God in Israel." How balanced was it for a young boy with no battle armor to go against a nine-foot warrior? How sensible was it? How wise? This was a zealous worshipper whose actions perfectly expressed the zeal of his songs to Yahweh.

In his book *The Barbarian Way*, Erwin McManus contrasts the radical lifestyle of the early followers of Jesus to the watered-down version of modern Christianity. When Christianity becomes too civilized, there isn't much talk of sacrifice and risk. Everyone is promised comfort, security, safety and prosperity. Says McManus:

> We have lost the simplicity of that raw, untamed, and primal faith ... Jesus is being lost in a religion bearing His name. People are being lost because they cannot reconcile Jesus' association with Christianity. Christianity has become docile, domesticated, civilized.
>
> The result and proof of faith are that you get to live a life without risk, which is ironic when you realize that for the early church, faith was a risky business ...
>
> The more you trust Him, the more you risk on His behalf. The more you love Him, the more you will love others. If you genuinely embrace His sacrifice, you will joyfully embrace a sacrificial life.*

---

* Erwin Raphael McManus, *The Barbarian Way: Unleash the Untamed Faith Within* (Thomas Nelson, 2005).

Abraham risked when he journeyed to the promised land; Paul risked when he turned away from his rabbinical tradition to follow Jesus; the disciples risked when they left the family business. All of this was done in the spirit of sacrificial worship.

It's not about trying to mimic someone else's life. If I look at biblical heroes and contemporary saints like Mother Teresa, and think of matching their accomplishments, I just get depressed. We should never be motivated by guilt. But that doesn't excuse us from using the faith and gifts God gives each one of us, whatever our resources.

It's important to mention that no single person or family in our church spends a huge amount of time reaching out to the needy; everyone has jobs and families that take up most of their time. But we can all make time to be a friend to someone who is oppressed, broken, lonely or disabled.

Following Jesus means attempting things we can't do in our own strength. Rick Warren has said, "If you've never attempted to do anything that you couldn't accomplish in your own strength, you've never had to exercise faith." He's right. We must not stay within the confines of our own strength: if we do, how will God have the chance to demonstrate that he is God in us and through us?

In our church plant, many of the people we are caring for are very different from us. Some of them speak other languages and come from other cultures, and others have been crippled by broken marriages and lives of addiction.

Only as we make ourselves vulnerable (as Jesus did) and take the humble posture of a learner can we relate to people who come from totally different backgrounds. It's not always comfortable. As Erwin McManus says, "God's will for us is less about our comfort than our contribution." The humility required to relate to unfamiliar people groups is the same kind of humility that gives rise to a song of worship.

I'm learning to take the risk of caring for people who can't return the favor. I'm learning that to "look after orphans and widows" (James 1:27) doesn't necessarily mean "converting orphans and widows." True religion is to give despite what you get back. It's a risk to pour out your love to severely broken people. Sometimes you feel you're pouring your life into a black hole. But the risk of faith means giving to "the least of our brothers" as if we were giving to Jesus himself. We've learned that ministering with the poor is a very slow, gradual process. It's all about relationship.

INTEGRITY

In the last thirty years, there has been exponential growth in the "industry" of worship recordings. It's a ministry that has grown into an industry. We have endless songs and recordings. In the contemporary Church, there is a huge appetite for good worship music. But if we become focused on music to the neglect of mercy and mission, we're missing God's heart – we become ingrown, narrow-sighted and imbalanced.

With the huge number of new worship recordings every year and the commercial sizzle that creates a buzz about "the next hot product," it's possible to forget what worship is really all about. We can end up becoming connoisseurs of worship music while missing God's heart for the poor. With any gift that God gives, the focus can shift away from God and towards the gift. The Church should pursue excellence in the arts, but wonderful songs can become the end-goal rather than a means of personal transformation that results in doing Jesus stuff.

Enjoying good worship music and the gifted artists who create great music can be life-changing for us and our churches, but it can also degenerate into mere consumerism and fan club membership. A church can make the mistake of catering to an entertainment-hungry society and labeling it "the worship that God desires," while forgetting about the street people within a block of the church's front doors.

I think the key is that each of us has a unique journey, calling and sphere of influence. Each of us must keep taking steps of faith, asking God, "Who can I help today?" Don't overload yourself with huge demands and expectations. Just find someone to care for. Walk through the doors God opens for you, whether it's the door of a single mother down the street or a door to India. Don't try to match someone else's ministry, but remember that you're called to "be an imitator of God."

In the last twenty years I've visited over twenty-five other countries on ministry trips of various kinds. One key moment for me in hearing God's call to the nations came when I was waiting for a dental appointment. Next to the dentist's was a travel agency. I wandered over to this shop and stopped in front of a large rack of travel brochures. The brochures advertised destinations all over the world. God said to me, "That's where I've called you to go." I realized he meant "everywhere." It made me weep. On another occasion God told me, "You are like seed in my hand; as a farmer scatters seed on his land I'm going to throw you out to the nations."

I don't mean to say that traveling to other countries is more valuable than caring for the poor widow on our own street — it's not. While I do visit some third-world countries, most of my itinerant ministry is to middle-class people. In some cases, the people I minister to work full time with the poor.

FINALLY

In 2002 our family went to Hong Kong for a three-month international adventure. At that time, our eight children ranged from fifteen years to three months old. Linda and I had always wanted to give our kids a taste of living in another country, and a chance to hang out with a mercy ministry in the trenches of helping the poor. I had visited Hong Kong several times to do worship and teaching for different events, and was invited by Jackie Pullinger to bring my whole family to stay at Shin Mun Springs, which is St. Stephen's primary residential facility for ministry. Jackie is from England and has been in Hong Kong for over forty years, building a ministry that has led thousands to Christ. These days she leads a large team of workers throughout Hong Kong and in several other countries throughout Asia.

This was the perfect opportunity for our family. We lived in a flat that was part of a complex of buildings filled with men who were new converts to Christ. Most of these men had been rescued out of drug addiction and weren't much more than skeletons when they first came for help to a St. Stephen's addicts meeting. Many had been members of dangerous gangs called the Triads.

Most of them had come from broken homes full of anger and fighting. Many of these men were beaten as children, and sometimes kicked out of the house at a very young age to fend for themselves.

Our role in the community was simply to be friends with these brothers. We ate most of our meals with them, worshipped with them and prayed for them. Our boys loved playing volleyball and soccer with the brothers, and going hiking and bike riding. I gave guitar lessons to many of the brothers, and taught worship workshops for the many worship leaders and teams throughout the city.

We did nothing heroic, just shared our time with the brothers. Before coming, Jackie kept telling me how wonderful it would be if we would simply come and live as a family among them. Just being an example of a healthy family was a healing experience for the brothers. Seeing a husband treat his wife and children with gentleness and respect was eye-opening for them. When my kids disobeyed and I didn't beat them, the brothers watched carefully.

I'm a task-oriented person — I like to see concrete results. So it was hard to believe that we were really contributing anything to the St. Stephen's brothers simply by carrying on normal family life. But what is normal life for us was a dream world for them. There was a world of difference compared to the painful family life they had known.

Also during these three months our family band played many times around the city — in parks, schools and apartment building courtyards. Our family plays the whole range of band instruments — bass, drums, guitars, keyboards and vocals. We played in a huge shopping center on Christmas Day. Once we played worship music in a jail for young people. The churches connected with St. Stephen's do outreaches all the time, so we just joined the party.

St. Stephen's is another ministry in which worship and mercy are all part of one big kingdom-of-God package. Rarely have I seen people worship with such passion as at St. Stephen's. The brothers and workers from around the world who come to serve are desperately hungry for God's presence and refueling. They know the only way they can effectively minister and continue the fight of faith is to draw near to God for empowering.

PRIVILEGE

Being a friend of God is the greatest privilege we could ever have. To worship him means to extend that friendship to those around us, including the poor.

Our sacrifice of worship is described in *The Message* like this: "Take your everyday, ordinary life – your sleeping, eating, going-to-work, and walking-around life – and place it before God as an offering . . . readily recognize what he wants from you, and quickly respond to it" (Romans 12:1–2).

If we see ourselves as seed that God can scatter however he chooses, to nourish and bless whoever he wants to, we'll be pleasing God with worship that is genuine.

LOOKING TO THE FUTURE

Graham and
Tamsin Kendrick

FIRST OF ALL, DAD, BEFORE WE GET TO THE FUTURE LET'S TALK ABOUT THE PAST . . . I HEAR YOU USED TO HAVE A BIG BEARD. WHAT HAPPENED TO IT?

I had a beard as soon as I was capable of growing one because it made me feel grown up. But it wasn't a very good one. The hippie movement was all about long hair, beards, wearing your granny's old fur coat with flowery shirts with outsize collars and ragged jeans. It was all very anti-establishment; it was just part of the massive social changes that were going on and the birth of youth culture. It was a very creative time, suddenly people were questioning the limits put on them by society.

DID THAT CREATIVITY MAKE IT EASIER OR HARDER TO TALK ABOUT GOD?

I think because people were questioning the status quo — and because the Church was seen as part of the establishment, the authority structure of society — it was definitely a time of questioning and challenging. Along with distrusting politicians, people would also question religious leaders and institutions, in a way they wouldn't have dared to in a previous generation. However, although we were questioning everything I still think we had quite a clear structure of right and wrong, good and bad. There were still rules of behavior and standards of good and bad, rooted in the Christian background of the nation. So it was a time of debate, but more and more from a defensive position because the tide of opinion had turned against what people perceived as Church and Christianity. People today talk about the "end of Christendom," in other words the end of the era when Christian-based ideas and laws were generally accepted as being true and right. We were experiencing a major sea change.

WHAT ABOUT YOU, DID YOU REBEL?

I think I took on a lot of the questioning attitude, and a certain degree of cynicism about the way things were, but at the same time I was really determined to find out what authentic Christianity was. That was the positive side of it for me. The institutions of religion were being questioned, and much of it needed to be questioned. But my reaction was to say: let's go back to the most authentic accounts of Christian faith, let's go back to the New Testament and see how our lives compare to those of the disciples and of Christ. Let's see how real that is. Let's see if that can be lived today.

BUT THOSE DAYS ARE SO DIFFERENT FROM THESE TIMES.

Yes and no; the rejection of historic Christianity and its teaching is much further advanced, but more than ever I think people want to see something authentic and real, something that works in experience, and especially that can be seen to work in the face of the big issues of the day, such as climate change and terrorism. We were more focused on the changes that were happening within the Church itself, but I see the Church today becoming much more engaged with wider issues and a waking up to the fact that although there seems to be such overwhelming suffering in the world, God is at work in powerful ways. This gives me so much hope for our future.

AND SO WHAT DID YOU GUYS DISCOVER ABOUT CHRISTIANITY?

I think the area of rediscovery in my generation, in my contexts or circles, was in two main areas. One was of church being a place where we could enjoy real relationships as opposed to just brushing shoulders with people in a pew every week. And the second one, but intimately connected to that, was the whole area of experience, of how much of what we saw in the New Testament we could expect to experience today. Does God heal today? Can we experience the Holy Spirit today? Can we see miracles today? And with those two things happening, we were probably less aware of the issues to do with justice and poverty. Moral issues tended to get more attention, because public morality was changing; it was the era of the contraceptive pill, and from the Church's perspective there was a lot of concern about the rejection of Christian morality, and then a lot of excitement about this new experience of the power and presence of God. So it took a while before this movement woke up to issues of justice and poverty.

WHAT KIND OF MUSIC WERE YOU WRITING BACK THEN?

For many years the kind of music I was involved with was more telling the salvation story. One of the things I was known for was writing songs that would take a character from the gospel or take a scene from the gospel and turn it into a narrative song.

SO SONGS QUITE DIFFERENT FROM "SHINE, JESUS, SHINE," THEN?

These weren't songs that people sang along with. These were concerts; this was when contemporary Christian music was coming alive. There would be concert tours and so on. Normally, for most non-conformist churches, their worship would be hymn-based, and then choruses would be used with the children and for after church meetings or week-night meetings which were more informal. These would be more sing-along times, more of a social bonding experience than one in which you would expect to connect with God in any great depth.

WHAT HAPPENED TO CHANGE THIS?

What was happening, particularly in the 1970s, was that the renewal movement began to spring up, all around the world, where people began to have deeper experiences of the Holy Spirit. And then the doctrine of the baptism of the Spirit began to be taught in many places, and when people entered into this deeper experience of the Holy Spirit it meant that they began to worship in a much more experiential way. Worship became more personal; we started to sing songs to God rather than about him. And there was an expectation that the worship would be shaped as it went along, by the guidance of the Holy Spirit and in many cases the use of the gifts of the Holy Spirit. As it says in 1 Corinthians 14:26, "What then shall we say, brothers? When you come together, everyone has a hymn, or a word of instruction, a revelation, a tongue or an interpretation. All of these must be done for the strengthening of the church."

SOUNDS LIKE IT COULD GET QUITE CONFUSING . . .

There were definitely times when I thought *I have no idea what is going on here.* Yet it was great: I think people began to have a renewed sense of what it might mean to be a community of believers where God was present in tangible ways. Worship began to be more this mixture of personal worship from the heart, songs sung to God, together with being open for people to bring their own contribution into the service. So it became less front-led, and more energized by what the people brought. So as a worship leader (the very concept of a worship leader was very new in those days in the way we understand it today) the role was more of leading these kinds of songs, and then responding to what was happening in the worship service. As you can imagine, with all these people bringing their own contributions, at times it could be very messy.

IF THAT WAS WHAT WORSHIP MUSIC NEEDED THEN, WHAT ABOUT NOW?

One of the things it needs is a restoration of some of those things that I've just described.

I think that many groups have adopted the method and style that grew from those times – that of stringing songs together to create an unbroken focus on the presence of God – but know little of the actual presence and power of God. But the danger that I see now is that in some places the only way that worship is perceived is as a personal individualistic experience. There's a tendency to seek some kind of sense of well-being and of being loved by God, to the exclusion of other people and of the needs of the world that we live in. I think we're in danger, if our sung worship becomes a way in which we escape from the realities of a broken world, rather than a place where we engage with its realities and receive a vision of how we can serve and make a difference. I think the key to it is to understand what true intimacy with God is.

SURELY GETTING INTIMATE WITH GOD MEANS LEAVING THIS WORLD BEHIND. AFTER ALL, IF GOD IS NON-PHYSICAL HOW CAN WE TOUCH HIM OTHERWISE?

I think this is often the mistake people make, thinking that God is up there somewhere, totally detached from the world. In fact, the wonder of our faith is that God has been revealed to us as one who loved the world so much that he actually became flesh and blood: the term used is "incarnation," becoming flesh and blood. So not only do we worship this amazing, humble, serving and suffering God, but we are called to offer our bodies for him to continue his ministry in and through this world. God is totally involved with his world, but he has chosen to get his hands dirty through ours, if we are willing to make them available.

ARE YOU SAYING WE CAN HAVE AN INTIMATE EXPERIENCE OF GOD DOING THE WASHING UP, OR TALKING TO A FRIEND?

I'm sure that is possible, but if the whole point is to have an experience of God and just spend it selfishly on ourselves, I think we have a problem. The word "intimacy" has been used, in many views of worship, to describe the arrival point of worship, the destination of worship, which is fine as long as we make sure we have defined intimacy with God in its full meaning.

DESTINATION? WHAT KIND OF DESTINATION?

The paradigm that is used – and, by the way, I think it is a good one – is the tabernacle that Moses built, and on which later temples were modeled, where there were several outer courts around an inner room where the presence of God was manifested in a special way, and where only the High Priest was allowed to enter once a year to offer incense on behalf of the Jewish nation. It was the place from which God would speak to Moses, face to face, as a friend, hence the idea of intimacy with God.

SO INTIMACY IS ABOUT FRIENDSHIP WITH GOD?

It is, but friendships are more than just having feelings of friendship, the experience of friendship. It's about the things that are important to your friend becoming important to you. Moses was intimate with God; God called him his friend. But Moses did not use his friendship with God to escape from the realities of the day-to-day problems that he faced leading the people of God. It was in that place of intimacy of friendship with God that he sought and found answers and where he got to know what God was like, and therefore how he viewed what was going on in the lives of the people and what should be done about it. The best example, of course, is Jesus, whom his disciples observed as having a tremendously intimate relationship with God, as he prayed "Abba Father," which basically means Daddy, or Dad – a very personal expression that probably would have shocked them in their religious culture.

IS IT THAT IN PRIVATE JESUS BEGAN TO FEEL HOW GOD WOULD FEEL, BUT THAT WASN'T COMPLETE UNTIL HE'D DONE SOMETHING ABOUT IT?

You could put it like that. Jesus went up the mountain to be alone with his Father but he came down the mountain and immersed himself in ministering to the needs of the people who flocked to him. We need a kind of worship that takes us up the mountain but also brings us down again, envisioned and empowered to do the works of the Father.

AH . . . SO OUT OF INTIMACY FLOWS MINISTRY?

Right. Out of Christ's intimacy with God flowed all the solid, practical things he did in the world. I've always been struck by the time when Jesus said that he did nothing of his own initiative, but only what he saw his Father doing. Whether he was up in the mountains praying through the night or walking among the people and moved to action because they were desperate and helpless, it was all an overflow of the same. Perhaps it was a healing, perhaps the feeding of the five thousand, deliverance from an evil spirit or a teaching that would move people to live differently.

HAVE YOU EVER EXPERIENCED THIS INTIMACY IN ACTION?

Well, I find that the only way I can minister effectively is to get close to God in prayer, and proceed on the basis of the direction I believe God gives me. Even though I may be in a familiar situation and using familiar material, I am always desperate to know what God may be wanting to do in particular, and I regularly find myself on the precipice of faith, stepping out and hoping that solid ground will appear under my feet just in time.

But a very different occasion comes to mind as well. As you know, I am an enthusiastic supporter of the work of Compassion. Before I went to India I was already a child sponsor with them, but my first child's family had moved to a different area, away from the project, leaving me "childless." Around the same time, however, I was invited on a trip to India to see several projects. The Compassion UK director suggested I might choose a child from one of these, which I thought might be a good idea.

SOUNDS SCARY. YOU HAD TO PICK ONE CHILD OUT TO HELP, AND LEAVE ALL THESE OTHERS BEHIND? I'M GLAD YOU DIDN'T HAVE TO PICK ME LIKE THAT!

Indeed. I didn't realize how difficult the choice would be, but I knew I couldn't help them all. The night before we were due to go, I was given a printout of passport-sized photos of about fifty unsponsored children from a particular village. As I sat in my hotel room looking at these children, I found it an impossible task, simply because just by choosing one I was not choosing the other forty-nine, who I guessed were just as needy.

AND GOD HELPED YOU?

Well, the only way I knew how to deal with it was to pray that in some way God would pick out a child for me. Yes, it was a bit like passing the buck, but although I knew that helping any of them would be a great result, I really did want to know that God was helping me, and perhaps even leading me to a particularly needy family.

Finally we arrived at the project, and when playground time came

I wandered round, ostensibly taking photographs but really looking for some clue, wondering how God would point a particular child out to me. I watched them play, praying all the time.

AND THEN YOU SPOTTED MARMONI . . . SORRY, GETTING A LITTLE AHEAD OF YOU THERE.

Yes. Then I spotted Marmoni. As I looked around, a particular girl in a red dress caught my eye. She seemed a little quieter than the others, a little bit on her own, so I watched her and began to pray. I'm quite shy myself, so perhaps I identified with her quietness. Also, as you know, you are one of four daughters, so choosing a girl seemed pretty natural as well.

AND THAT'S WHEN YOU FELT THAT INTIMACY WITH GOD?

All I can say is that my heart was moved in such a way that I believed I was experiencing a little touch of God's love for this particular child. And so I chose. It was only later, when, together with some of the project workers, she took us to her home – which was just a tarpaulin over mud walls – that it became evident that she was one of the most needy children in the village. Her father had become disabled and could not work to support his wife and five children, and that was only one of their problems.

SO, JESUS' INTIMACY WITH THE FATHER WAS NOT ABOUT ESCAPING FROM THE PROBLEMS OF THE WORLD, IT WAS A PATHWAY TO ENGAGING WITH THE PROBLEMS OF THE WORLD?

Yes, if intimacy never leads to action then we have to question whether we are close to God at all. In fact, I have begun to see that this is not really about us deciding to do something good or loving or merciful, but rather it is about the privilege of being invited to participate in our heavenly Father's loving actions.

WOW, THAT SOUNDS A BIT COMPLEX. SAY IT AGAIN, DAD.

It all flows out of an understanding that whether we worship God in word or deed, it is all made possible through Christ. There are a beautiful pair of definitions that I love, penned by the theologian James Torrance, that have helped me grasp this at least a little bit. The first is to do with worship, when he explains: "worship is the gift of participating through the Spirit in the incarnate Son's communion with the Father."

The second is to do with the way we serve God's world: "The mission of the church is nothing less than the gift of sharing by the Spirit in the Son's mission to the world on behalf of the Father." The amateur theologian in me gets excited at this Trinitarian pattern. Approaching God in worship, and serving him in the world is made possible by all that Christ achieved through his life, death, resurrection and ascension. In the end, none of it is our work, nor could it be. We see again in John 20:21, after the resurrection when Jesus appeared to his disciples, he said: "Peace be with you! As the Father has sent me, I am sending you."

OK, I THINK I UNDERSTAND. SO IF WE BELONG TO THE CHURCH AND WE ARE NOT ENGAGING IN ISSUES OF JUSTICE, THEN WE DON'T REALLY HAVE A RELATIONSHIP WITH GOD?

I wouldn't put it quite like that because the term "engaging in issues of justice" could be used by different people to mean many different things. My all-time favorite definition of a worshipper, in other words a person whose actions flow out of relationship with God, can be found in the writings of the Apostle Paul. After describing all kinds of loving behavior and its opposite in the preceding verses, he encourages his readers with the words: "Be imitators of God, therefore, as dearly loved children and live a life of love, just as Christ loved us and gave himself up for us as a fragrant offering and sacrifice to God" (Ephesians 5:1). In the culture in which he wrote, offerings and sacrifices were the imagery of worship, and here he is describing a life of love and self-giving.

There are numerous ways to express love, and caring about justice and poverty is among the loving, God-imitating actions that we should seek to do. Another New Testament writer and close friend of Jesus, called John, states quite bluntly: "If anyone says, 'I love God,' yet hates his brother, he is a liar. For anyone who does not love his brother, whom he has seen, cannot love God, whom he has not seen" (1 John 4:20). Some of the best "imitators of God" I have known would never have thought of what they did in terms of engaging in issues of justice, but actually by loving and serving those around them in Christ's name, that's what they were doing.

DO YOU THINK THAT OUR CURRENT WORSHIP SONGS HELP US TO ENGAGE WITH THE ISSUE OF JUSTICE?

Well, certainly some do but we could do with a whole lot more. I think that since this emphasis on feeling close to and loved by God in the act of worship, we now have a lot of songs that facilitate that but not many that take us to other places and other aspects of God's character and nature. In some places there is a default worship style, which seems to exclude anything that doesn't take us to a personal expression of loving God and being loved. Now there's nothing wrong with this in itself, but my question is, have we marginalized other important aspects of engaging with God?

DO YOU THINK GOD EVER SITS THERE AND THINKS, "WHAT ARE YOU DOING? THAT'S NOT HOW IT'S SUPPOSED TO BE DONE"?

I am astounded at how God puts up with us at all. No wonder he is described as slow to anger and quick to show mercy. But there is one notable outburst through the prophet Amos about some worship songs that God hated. I must admit I was a little shocked when I first came across it. After all, if his people have gone to the trouble of meeting together to give him glory, it seems a bit much if they then discover he doesn't like it.

HANG ON, I THOUGHT GOD WAS SUPPOSED TO LOVE OUR . . . WELL, LOVE SONGS TO HIM?

Well, although he cries out: "Take away the noise of your songs!" I don't think his complaint is against a particularly bad batch of songs, a rubbish PA system or incompetent musicians. Amos says,

> I hate, I despise your religious feasts;
> I cannot stand your assemblies . . .
> Away with the noise of your songs!
> I will not listen to the music of your harps.
> But let justice roll on like a river,
> righteousness like a never-failing stream.
> Amos 5:21–24

SOUNDS A BIT HARSH.

Yes, but what had happened to that community was that they had fallen into the age-old trap of divorcing their religion from their daily lives, their songs and prayers from their domestic, social and business relationships. The river of justice had run dry, the stream of righteousness was reduced to stagnant pools. As a result their worship, though perhaps professionally done, aesthetically satisfying and artistically inspiring, had become an offensive cacophony in the ears of a just and righteous God.

IT'S A KIND OF LYING TO GOD?

It's singing something that is contradicted by your actions. The beauty of the prayers, songs and music or the dignity or solemnity of religious services do not in themselves please God. God is looking for a deeper kind of music, a richer kind of liturgy: the music of our obedience, and the daily liturgy of loving our neighbor. Lips and life need to agree.

OK. SO WHAT ABOUT THE ISSUE OF POVERTY? HAVE YOU BEEN DELIBERATELY WRITING MORE SONGS ABOUT THAT RECENTLY?

Yes, I have, though I don't have a master plan of what I'm going to write about — it tends to be more intuitive than that. I might be writing a song in response to what's happening in my local church, or I might be asked to write on a particular theme or see a need for a song on a particular theme.

I've definitely become more aware in recent years of the need to bring issues of poverty and justice into songs, but also of the challenge of doing that without getting heavy, or leaving everyone feeling condemned, guilty or depressed.

I KNOW YOU SPEND A LOT OF TIME READING THE PSALMS; DO THEY HELP YOU WHEN YOU DECIDE WHAT TO WRITE ABOUT?

I think if we're looking for balance of subject matter the psalms are the place to go, and in fact I think you can argue that they should rightly be taken as a model of the range of subjects that we should be vocalizing in Christian worship.

ARE THERE ANY PSALMS YOU CAN USE TO EXPLAIN THIS?

There are loads. One particularly good example that relates to this conversation is Psalm 113.

> Praise the LORD.
> Praise, O servants of the LORD,
> praise the name of the LORD.
> Let the name of the LORD be praised,
> both now and for evermore.
> From the rising of the sun to the place where it sets,
> the name of the LORD is to be praised.
>
> The LORD is exalted over all the nations,
> his glory above the heavens.
> Who is like the LORD our God,
> the One who sits enthroned on high,
> who stoops down to look
> on the heavens and the earth?

He raises the poor from the dust,
and lifts the needy from the ash heap;
he seats them with princes,
with the princes of their people.
He settles the barren woman in her home,
as a happy mother of children.

Praise the LORD.

SO WHAT DO YOU SEE IN PARTICULAR IN THIS ONE?

While being quite a short psalm, it has an amazing span to it; it is a psalm of praise that begins by describing a God so great that he looks down even upon the galaxies. It reminds me of the amazing photographs that have been beamed down from the Hubble telescope which show the sheer hugeness and splendor of the universe. Then suddenly the scene changes to him reaching down into the rubbish heap and lifting up the poor and seating them with princes. This is a fantastic picture of the extremes of God: God the almighty Creator and yet the God who gets personally involved with the poorest of the poor. And though this psalm was written many hundreds of years before Christ it's easy to see a foreshadowing of the incarnation – how God in Christ physically did that very thing.

SO WE HAVE THE MEEKNESS AND MAJESTY OF GOD . . . HEY, THAT SOUNDS STRANGELY FAMILIAR. ANYTHING ELSE THE PSALMS TELL US WE SHOULD BE SINGING ABOUT?

There are many songs today that give us an excellent language for expressing our personal love and thanks to God, but the psalms also give us a language for anger, for frustration that the world is not as it should be, for protesting against injustice and for lamenting the tragedies that we see around us. We need to rediscover some of this language in our worship music today. We need to write songs that allow the Christian community to grieve, protest or lament. I was struck recently by a quote from Walter Brueggemann: "The Psalter knows that life is dislocated. No cover-up is necessary. The Psalter is a collection over a long period of time of the eloquent, passionate songs and prayers of people who are at the desperate edge of their lives."*

THAT *COULD* SOUND QUITE DEPRESSING: SHOULDN'T CHURCH BE A PLACE THAT LIFTS OUR SPIRITS, NOT BRINGS US DOWN?

I think the language of worship should reflect the realities of life but infused with the amazing hope of the gospel. It is not just the world "out there" that is struggling: every worshipping community has its share of sickness and suffering. We need to write and sing songs that deal with all of these, but lift us up in hope to the God who in his incarnate Son has suffered with us, is with us now in the person of the Holy Spirit to help us, and who will bring us safely to his kingdom where there is no longer suffering, sorrow or death.

YOU'RE SAYING THAT SADNESS HAS A PLACE IN WORSHIP? I THOUGHT EVERYBODY WAS SUPPOSED TO JUMP ABOUT AND BE HAPPY?

I think sometimes that should definitely be the case, but it is not just a choice of happy or sad. There is a place to be dissatisfied, even angry with the way things are, and for a desperate longing to see the world restored to how God intended it to be. I remember Bishop Graham Cray quoting the German theologian Jürgen Moltmann: "Those who hope in Christ can no longer put up with reality as it is, they begin to suffer

* Walter Brueggemann, *Praying the Psalms* (second edition, Cascade Books, 2007).

under it, contradict it. Peace with God means conflict with the world, for the goad of God's promised future stabs inexorably, relentlessly into the flesh of every unfulfilled moment."*

WE DON'T HAVE TO WALK AROUND WITH A PLASTERED SMILE ON OUR FACE, THEN?

Not all the time, though if you were constantly miserable I would be concerned. Christ has given us this vision of the kingdom of heaven, and so we should not be happy with the world around us.

WHAT MIGHT THAT KINGDOM LOOK LIKE?

There are some beautiful prophetic glimpses in the scriptures. Isaiah gives us several, and I especially love the bit in the book of Revelation where John hears a voice announce: "Now the dwelling of God is with men, and he will live with them. They will be his people, and God himself will be with them and be their God. He will wipe every tear from their eyes. There will be no more death or mourning or crying or pain, for the old order of things has passed away" (Revelation 21:3–4).

Our hearts need to express this hope and longing in worship, to ask God how long before the world can truly be redeemed. You see, a lot of Christians think – and this is a very Graeco-Platonic idea – that when we die we somehow become souls floating in a heaven of clouds and ethereal music.

I GET THE BIT ABOUT THE CLOUDS, BUT GRAECO-WHAT?

I'm talking about the Greek philosophy that was largely based on the

* Jürgen Moltmann, *Theology of Hope* (HarperCollins, 1990).

philosopher Plato's ideas about humanity. I think, from that, Western Christianity has somehow borrowed the notion that we are sort of souls trapped in bodies. That being physical is bad and one day we will just be spirits floating around in the sky.

OK. SO WHAT DOES THAT HAVE TO DO WITH LONGING FOR A BETTER FUTURE?

I think that when Christians think that everything physical will be destroyed, they perhaps care less about looking after the world for the future, because maybe they think it won't be around for too long. But this is not what the Bible teaches us at all. The Bible teaches us that we will have a full physical resurrection, as Christ did. That his resurrection was just the beginning of the liberation of the whole creation from death and decay, and its renewal.

BUT DIDN'T CHRIST WALK THROUGH WALLS AND MAGICALLY DISAPPEAR AND THINGS? THAT DOESN'T SOUND TOO PHYSICAL TO ME!

But he also ate and drank, showed his wounds to Thomas and was a physical and whole person. Jesus ascended to heaven in a physical body – a glorified and transformed one, to be sure, but a physical body. When he resurrected he didn't just disintegrate back into God, and we are told that we will become like him when we are resurrected.

SO CHRIST SORT OF DID IT FIRST, TO SHOW US HOW IT IS DONE?

I think the message is that we will be caught up in his resurrection; this is the hope we need to have inside us. That beautiful promise of God's: behold! I make all things new. Not just your body but also the body of the world.

OK THEN, SO EVERYTHING WILL BE MADE NEW, BUT THERE WILL BE NO MORE SUFFERING AND WE'LL BE ABLE TO WALK THROUGH WALLS?

I'm not sure about the walking through walls or quite what purpose that would serve, but the end of suffering and death, and the "all things made new" is very clear.

This hope is what enables us to work long term rather than look for quick-fix situations. Ministering to the poor not only meets someone's need here and now, it is of eternal value because it is serving Christ and he is eternal. Feeding the poor now is building the eternal kingdom of God, and even if we seem to fail or experience disappointment it is a sign of what is to come, a taste of the future. We need songs that give voice to that hope which will sustain us in difficult times.

DO YOU THINK THAT WORSHIP SHOULD BE ABOUT THE FUTURE?

It's about the past, present and future. It's about retelling and remembering what the Lord has done, as Moses and Miriam do in Exodus 15, praising him for delivering his people. But it is also about encountering God now in the present and anticipating the fullness of his kingdom in the future. In worship we should be retelling the story of our salvation and having a present encounter with God through the Spirit, but perhaps one of the neglected themes is the anticipation of the completion of what was begun and promised at the resurrection: a new world where there will be no more suffering, where we will walk with God in a world free from hunger, disease and abuse. Sometimes it is hard to believe in that vision of the future, but as Jim Wallis said, "Faith is believing in God, despite the evidence. Then watching the evidence change before your eyes."

DOESN'T PAUL SAY SOMETHING LIKE THAT?

Paul says in Hebrews 11 that faith is being sure of what we hope for and certain of what we do not see. Faith, however small it is, is not based on today. Faith lives in the future. Someone once said that faith is hearing the music of the future and dancing to it now.

WE NEED TO BRING THIS TO AN END NOW; DO YOU HAVE ANY FINAL WORDS?

I think I express things best in song lyrics, so is it OK to quote a few lines?

OH, GO ON THEN . . .

Thanks, daughter. This is from the last verse of "Crucified Man," a song about the apparent foolishness of putting your hope in a man dying on a cross:

> I have buried my life in the cold earth with him
> Like a seed in the winter, I wait for the spring
> From that garden of tombs, Eden rises again
> And Paradise blooms from his body
> And never will end
> He'll finish all he began
> Creation hopes in a crucified man
> > From "Crucified Man" by Graham Kendrick.*

* Graham Kendrick. © 2006 Make Way Music www.grahamkendrick.co.uk

MY ALLERGIC REACTION

Stu Garrard

COMFORT, COMFORT, COMFORT, COMFORT. EVERYWHERE I LOOK THE SAME THING: THE PULLS AND THE TEMPTATIONS TO EASE MYSELF INTO A WAY OF LIVING THAT'S EASIER, SOFTER AND JUST PLAIN COMFORTABLE.

My food promises to cause me less stress, my phone network suggests that I could do with a break and treat myself to an easier way of operating, my bank wants to help out and take my mind off the day-to-day and sort me out with a loan so that I can treat myself to a big holiday or an even bigger car.

I settle myself on the sofa, summon the remotes and allow myself to drift into a film. I see some perfect couple having the perfect marriage with the perfect absence of hard work and tedious self-sacrifice. If only life were this comfortable ...

The magazines all add to the noise, telling me that I can have it all — that in some way I *deserve* it all. Why? Because here in the wealthy West the life that is marked by ease and instant hits and minimal stress and strife is held up as being the best we could possibly aim for.

It's not just the cash or the relationships that we get duped by. Faith has been comforted up too: those rough edges and hard truths smoothed over. We've been told that we can retreat into a world populated solely by our own kind, that we can leave those awkward questions at the door and simply sign up to a set of beliefs that fall into line behind the rest. We've been told that we can have it all – or 90 percent of it, at least. We've been told that we can explore faith without having to really spend too much time worrying about what it should mean for our life from Monday to Saturday. We've ignored the bits that suggest that following Christ will challenge our sense of comfort. Instead, we've signed up for a faith that makes us more comfortable, not less.

♥

I'm sorry about that. But I just had to get it off my chest. I'm a guitarist – playing music is how I make sense of things. Whenever I have to write I seem to end up with a touch of chaos and too many false starts. So I'll try again. . .

I've been thinking a lot about the way that we live these days. It's the way that *I* live that first got my attention – the realization that it's a little too far away from what I see in the life of Jesus than I'd like.

Lately we've been hearing about the kingdom of God. I'm not sure I can easily define it, but I know that it has something to do with living a whole life, something to do with getting out beyond the hollow and the religious and seeing God transform the world for the better. It has something to do with a place where God is king. But instead of God's kingdom I get the feeling that there are plenty of us who have spent a whole load more time building our own Kingdom of Comfort.

When I think about the Kingdom of Comfort I think about two things. The first is that it describes the decisions that we take to build our castle and homes. We make these choices, about what material possession to acquire next, under the illusion that we do it in isolation. We don't for one minute assume that the latest games console arriving at our house will have an impact on anyone else on the other side of the world. I see this all throughout my own life – the way I make a couple of clicks on the mouse and buy whatever it is that I want, with zero thought for the consequences of my actions. So I build my kingdom bit by bit, click by click, all the time making the walls higher and blocking myself in.

Then there's the other side to the Kingdom of Comfort. With the band I've been fortunate enough to have seen certain things. I've felt and tasted the extremes of wealth and poverty, and I've been left with my head spinning in my hands. I've been left feeling unable to change any of the chaos and poverty, but I've felt completely convinced that I need to try. At the very least I need to ask myself some hard questions: am I responsible for any of this inequality and oppression in the world? And am I responsible for making it better? And how do I do that, living as I do in a completely average town that people move to when they're ready to think about dying? And how do I change the world when I'm a guy with a wife and two kids and a dog and a mortgage? Aren't these the sorts of problems that the radicals without all the responsibilities take on?

And I guess that's where the journey begins to start trying to find some answers. I don't think it does have to be that way – that ordinary people from ordinary towns with ordinary concerns are powerless to make a difference. And I don't think that my faith has to be all inward-looking. And I don't think that my life will only be a success if I manage to make myself as comfortable as possible.

★

I was in Cambodia and India last summer. My family were with me and we saw things that made us laugh, things that made us retch, things that left us speechless and things that left us with empty prayers but full hearts. We saw a lot on that trip and lived every minute of it knowing that we were living through days that were becoming part of our history. And then we flew home and moved house – to a bigger, more expensive home, with a bigger, more expensive mortgage and a bigger, far more heavy sense of guilt.

Feeling like hypocrites, we faced a choice. Retreat back into the world of comfort, put our heads back under the duvet and soothe the questions and the awkwardness away? Not this time. This time we decided to face up to the fact that life didn't quite make sense, to look at the state we're in and not try and ignore it all.

Things I saw when I looked bothered me. I realized that I was beginning to feel uncomfortable with my faith, uncomfortable with the way that too often it seems to be used to divide up and polarize the world into what we like and what we don't, into them and us.

We have our own music, our own books, our own TV, our own clothing, our own holidays and our own science. None of them in themselves are intrinsically wrong – no more wrong than the courses and clubs that exist for golfers, or the venues and music that exist for people who wear cowboy hats and who drive pick-up trucks. But the one thing that gets me when I make those comparisons is that while everyone might not be into golf or country music, everyone has a soul. I'm guessing that swinging a five iron around on a hot afternoon is not a massive factor when it comes to determining the fate of your soul, and learning how to line-dance isn't exactly going to lift lives out of the agonies of poverty. But Christianity – following Christ – aims for a far higher outcome than golf or country music. How can we really be connected with the world when so much of what we do separates us? How can we hope to be understood when we have our own language? How can we hope for people to want to join us when we make them clones rather than disciples?

So this is my journey. I'm trying to work out what church actually is. Or, more importantly, what following Jesus actually means. I'd forgotten that he surrounded himself with the poor, that he was part of a repressed culture living under a first-century superpower, that life was hard and real and messy. Instead, I'd read my Bible in other ways. I'd taken Jesus' words as if they had been written just for me, just for now. OK, so I know that all scripture is valid and worthy, but I'm now asking the question: is taking it all at face value, is taking it literally, always the right thing to do? There's an ancient culture to understand, and it's doing that which helps bring out the flavors and the genius of the writing.

So much of the time I spend in churches is colored by feelings that are confused. I love the communities that I am connected to, and I am proud of the way that — at our best — we support and carry each other through the hardest of life's trials. But I often find myself looking around and wondering just how we ended up with all this jargon and weird little rituals and single-track ways of thinking about things. When did we ever decide that church worked best when we all sat down and listened in silence rather than discussed and debated the issues? When did we conclude that it didn't really matter so much if people didn't understand the way we talk, as they'd pick up what it meant to be "washed in the blood" or "pressing in after the Lord" soon enough?

But not now. I've met so many different people living godly lives, people I've seen God in, that I've had to question whether my way really is the only way. I'm an evangelical charismatic, and a lot of our thinking has formed in the last two hundred years as opposed to the last two thousand. Yet over the last eighteen months I've been slowly learning that it's OK to ask questions. And it's OK to expect answers to be found in unexpected places. And it's OK to feel uncomfortable with the answers. And it's OK to challenge a lifetime of preconceived ideas by learning more about God from a Catholic monk, a Jewish rabbi and an Anglican bishop.

THE CATHOLIC MONK

I don't remember all that much about why we were there, but when we arrived to play at a gig in Vienna a year or so ago I didn't expect things to end up being quite so eventful.

I was walking through the building and I saw this guy sitting down. He looked odd, but in an interesting and kind of familiar way. He was wearing a gray tunic, had short hair, a long beard and glasses. By my guess he was in his early forties, but despite that I was convinced he was some aging singer I'd been watching a documentary about – a guy formerly known as Cat Stevens who now goes by the name of Yusuf Islam.

I took a second look and realized that I was wrong, it wasn't Yusuf, but by this time I was pretty intrigued so I went and sat next to him. It turned out that this wasn't an aging hippie with a weird name: this was a bona fide Catholic monk. Better still, he'd just come off a forty-day fast in the wilderness. And I mean the literal wilderness – European style: on a mountainside, in a hut. No electricity, no running water, no food, no nothing, just a hut and a mountain. I was hooked.

His name was Brother Johannes, and he was the one who, a few years previously, had started the festival at which we were playing. I couldn't stop asking him about his fast in the wilderness and he told me all he could. He explained how for the first two weeks the experience was hellish. Brother Johannes didn't really like the dark, he told me, and his mind kicked into a strange gear, playing videotapes of every-thing he had done wrong in his life, right back from his misspent youth, before he became a monk at seventeen.

But the last ten days, they were something else. They were soaked, properly soaked, with the presence of Jesus. The lines between phys-ical and spiritual blurred, life and light mixed and by the end he was convinced that if he didn't drag himself down from the mountain he would end up getting absorbed up into heaven, just like the 365-year-old Enoch way back in Genesis.

The life of a Catholic monk is fascinating. Brother Johannes and his community spend much of their time in silence, whether it is while they are carrying out their tasks, eating their meals or attending to their devotions. However, every afternoon Brother Johannes goes into a place called the speaking room. It's close to the street and anyone — regardless of doctrine or faith — can go in. It's not a confession booth, but it is a place where people talk while the monks listen and talk back if the words are right.

I thought it was brilliant. Anything to do with the Church making it possible for ordinary people outside it to come in and get genuine, loving help gets me excited. Anything that is real and that connects Christians with their wider community — rather than make either of them feel alienated and dislocated — leaves me excited. Brother Johannes was inspiring — utterly inspiring.

At the end of our conversation I asked him to come and take communion with us. He said he'd pray, but he wouldn't come and share the sacraments. I worried that I'd offended him and said so. He laughed. I don't think I did, but his response was something I will never forget: the things that unite us are greater than those which divide us.

THE RABBI

When my family and I were in India last year, we found ourselves having lunch with our hosts, waiting for their uncle to show up. He happened to be a rabbi and I was keeping an eye out for some Hasidic-looking guy – all black suit and trilby with white shirt and curls. But I was wrong.

In stepped this loud American who was great fun. We started to talk. Actually, I started to talk. I'd just read a book by another rabbi called Lawrence Kushner and I was still excited by it – *Jewish Spirituality: A Brief Introduction For Christians* – and I told him how much I'd enjoyed it.

"Oh, Larry!" he said, "he's one of my best friends!" Turns out he is, too.

Anyway, this rabbi we were with – Rabbi Joseph Edelheit – he was from Minnesota and he'd been a synagogue rabbi for thirty years, only he was forced to stop a few years back when he had a heart attack and desperately needed to rethink his work–life balance. Like so many church leaders his life had been out of control: over two thousand families under his care and never any time for a day off. It was all too much on his body. So after his heart bypass he was told by his doctor that he faced a choice: quit running the synagogue or face more of the same – or worse.

Rabbi Joseph Edelheit ended up teaching Jewish studies at St. Cloud State University in Minnesota, soon becoming head of religious studies.

We spent quite a bit of time together and have kept on communicating since then. What gets me about him is how utterly inspiring his relationship with God is. Oh, and the other thing that gets me is that our friendship is a little tricky, since Jesus is not a savior to him. I can understand people raising their eyebrows here, but there's no denying either his knowledge or his obvious relationship with God. He has plenty to teach me, like a relative from way back in the past: our lives may have taken different directions over the years, but Rabbi Joseph is someone who knows a whole lot about the history that we share. It's a huge gift that he is capable of telling me about the past and makes me wonder about the present.

One of the things I've gleaned from Rabbi Joseph is how God is everywhere. I know it sounds stupid, wide-eyed and naïve, but it's not a Sunday school concept. It's a matter of us taking time to find God in life, about us being aware of his breadth, and it's been a revelation.

Old stories have taken on new life, like the episode where Moses confronted the burning bush. As a shepherd, Moses would have seen fires out in the tinder-dry scrubland before, but the fact that he noticed this one particular bush wasn't burning up is what makes this worth noting. This is a classic story for a Jewish rabbi, one that speaks of the importance of taking time to look at what might appear mundane or trivial or just nature doing its thing. Out of that seemingly "typical" incident Moses found God in a way that would have implications for the entire shape of the future. "Take off your shoes because this is holy ground": God's words are full of mystery and power, and perhaps it's not quite the case that the particular piece of ground was itself holy – it's not that we should now concern ourselves with tracking it down and building a shrine on it. What counts is that we learn that all that God has created – all this ground and dirt and dust – is holy, if we only open our eyes.

Talking like that makes faith bigger.

Things have been getting practically different too, since meeting Rabbi Joseph. He told us about how he and his family – along with countless other Jews around the world – gather every Friday at sundown. It's the start of the Sabbath, as Jewish days run from evening to morning, as described by the creation poem in Genesis. So the Sabbath actually finishes at sundown on Saturday. Anyway, they all congregate around a big table weighed down with great food. The front door is opened and anyone can come in – neighbors, children's friends, Jew and non-Jew alike. They bless the food, they bless his wife for making it, they bless the children and they bless the time. The meals can go on for hours: stories, laughter, recollection and relationship all bonding and blurring together. They remember things about themselves and their history in that particular time. They remember how God is a God out of time – beyond it, bigger than it, uncontained by it.

Something as simple as this has changed our lives – not just our thinking. We're going to have more dinner parties, we're going to spend more time with people, and when we eat we're going to stop what we're doing and savor the moments and the conversation, experiencing our own expression of Shabbat.

Trying to rediscover the art of stopping what we're doing and being aware of what's going on in life, of savoring the moment and reminding ourselves of where we've come from is hard – or harder than it should be. It's not something we're used to. We've missed so much of the art of living; we've made it something that needs to be a success, something that we know we've done well at because of the material trophies we've collected. Our Western culture is dominated by numbers and budgets and all those tangible marks of success that try to hide the messy truth that lies beneath. But the fact remains that if God is everywhere and a God of time and moments, then he's in the mess and the trouble; he's in the rest and the moments when we pause more than when we're trying to cram our heads with tasks and distractions. For me, this brings yet more excitement and more faith.

THE BISHOP

I got to know him – Graham Cray – over the years at Greenbelt, Britain's largest Christian arts festival. He'd be there, all beard and sandals with socks, but with the sharpest insight into what had been going on in the world of music over the previous year. And I don't mean any of the music that I'd been making. He was – and is – a man who constantly turned us around to look out from ourselves to the wider world beyond.

Each year he'd blow me away with his depth of knowledge and the insight of his analysis. A few years later he became head of Ridley Hall, Cambridge, a Church of England training college. He always called it the vicar factory, but the joke was that he was one man who was never going to create a bunch of clones. Later Graham became a bishop and we've spent more time with him as a band, firing questions that we've always struggled to answer: we don't know what we are – are we here just to help people to sing songs in church or do we have a place in the theatres and clubs?

For me, spending time with Bishop Graham has been a return to and a fresh revelation of the importance of turning back the clock and exploring rituals that may have long since vanished. I'm all about finding new expressions and getting excited by new experiences, but these rituals – the ancient ones – inspire me.

My great friend Jon and I will always try and hunt down the prayer chapels of cathedrals or churches whenever we're in some European city. Knowing that thousands of people have walked across the stones and sat and prayed on the ageless wood gets me inspired and determined to try to discover God in the moment.

So Bishop Graham represents something larger than my small experience of Christianity. He's a link with the past, another huge reason why I'm straining my eyes to look back beyond the last couple of centuries to see how our ancestors made sense of Christianity back before the days of internet access and credit cards. I know that the Anglican Church came out of the mess and stained ego of Henry VIII and his desire for a divorce – but at the same time the person that he used to form the services and prayer books, Thomas Cranmer, was a great Protestant theologian. I'm convinced that God had his hand on it all, guiding, steering, sculpting the ancient into the modern.

I trust Bishop Graham, and I trust the lessons that we can learn from the past. I trust the ritual and the uniforms, and I trust the fact that in times of national crisis – like the death of Princess Diana – people turn back to the guys in robes and dog-collars in search of something solid, ancient and eternal to cling to.

If I'm honest, there's something else about the structure and order of the Church of England that I find reassuring. In these days of megachurches and multi-million-dollar building programs, I sometimes worry that we're taking on board too much of our cultural identity from the mainstream Western empire. I like the fact that the Anglican Church is uncool, that the buildings are old and the uniforms out of time. OK, so cathedrals are impressive, but for their architecture and age more than their bling and youth.

I'm not sure that we ought to be trying so hard to make our churches attractive, or cool, or powerful. It's always seemed to me that God is far greater than each of those traits. I've been to a lot of churches that are attractive, cool and powerful – they have helped me, and

I've found many wonderful friends among them. But all that wealth and weight and size . . . does it seem like the kind of efficient, insurgent, nuisance-creating, mustardseed-like way that Jesus or the early Church got around to doing things? I am impressed with how much money and expertise is given to help the poor and needy, so I cannot be judgmental, and I really don't have any answers to it at all, but somehow I have to admit that it's something that makes me itch: are we in danger of believing our own hype? What I do know is that even a few thousand pounds can save many, many lives. CompassionArt does that: giving with maximum efficiency for maximum return, and I'm so happy to be a part of this because twelve songwriters from different backgrounds and parts of the Church remind me that it's not all about "me," that we need the big and the small, and if we work together to "do justice and walk humbly" then we will make a difference.

I admit it: I'm a hypocrite. I can make judgments without knowing the whole story – we are all doing our best – but I feel uncomfortable. I'm trying for excellence in my calling and vocation as a musician, so I can understand the concert stages and the expensive building programs, but I don't feel comfortable. And I feel *most* uncomfortable about some of the choices *I've* made, too. I feel uncomfortable about the fact that I take on board certain scriptures and not others. The "go back and sell all you have and give it to the poor" is one that I filter and analyze and interpret in context so much that I completely rob it of any power over my life.

That's why I'm learning to trust the ancient a little more than the modern. Somehow time gets to be an efficient filter of some of our worst impulses. As my friend Rabbi Joseph says, a good place to dwell is somewhere between the questions and the answers. If we have all the answers it's too black and white, with no room for maneuver and true dialogue.

♥

The monk, the rabbi and the bishop: they've all lent me their compass, all helped me on my journey. Brother Johannes taught me that God is accessible, but also that he is to be found away from all that is current and plastic, up on a mountain or in a room just off the high street.

Rabbi Joseph opened my mind to a bigger view of God, to the lost culture that we are so clearly missing, to the fact that with some clearer glasses I can get a far better view of much of this faith.

And then there's Bishop Graham. The strength and power and wealth of history has transformed me from someone feeling restless and frustrated with charismatic evangelicalism to a Christian who is learning that our roots aren't shallow, that the past offers many guides and lessons to appreciate.

So this is a journey that I'm on; towards connecting with people, away from that which is plastic and soulless in my culture, out toward the wealth of a broader culture, of finding new rituals but also acknowledging the wealth of the past. This is my journey, and the steps I am taking may be small and unsure, but I love them all the same.

★

I need to end now, but I'll just add in this last thought. I can be accused of being a bit all over the place – in my thinking and my approach to faith. And I wonder about the guy who buried the cash in the parable of the talents. The safest thing for all of us to do would be to stick in the center ground, to forget any ideas of moving out and pushing the boundaries, to just sit on these questions and gut feelings about where we're going. But staying still isn't enough; playing it safe isn't the way that this faith was born.

Psalm 61 says it all:

> Hear my cry, O God;
> listen to my prayer.
>
> From the ends of the earth I call to you,
> I call as my heart grows faint;
> lead me to the rock that is higher than I.
>
> For you have been my refuge,
> a strong tower against the foe.
>
> Psalm 61:1–3

We wander out – to the ends of the earth: it's where we've been sent, after all. And we'll find some of our journeys hard: some confusing, some unexpected. Neither is a sign of failure. Each is an opportunity to do "small things with great love," as Mother Teresa said: to call out for a guide to take us to the rock that is higher than each of us, the God who never changes, who protects and guides and sends us out again, back out to the ends of the earth, back out on our journeys beyond ourselves.

FIVE QUESTIONS
I WANT TO ASK

Israel Houghton

QUESTION 1: WHAT'S ALL THIS STUFF WE HAVE FOR, ANYWAY?

I never really had a sounding board around me to bounce my ideas off, but a few years back I was starting to wonder about things. What's the point of all this, of getting a stage and a microphone, of gaining access to people with the power to change things? Could it be that maybe, just maybe, the answer doesn't lie exclusively in my own hands? Could it be that all of this wealth and time and possibility is for something bigger than myself?

Could it be that the whole purpose of worship is more than music for the sake of music, that it's about more than having a great church experience? Could there be a Part 2 to all this?

Like so many of us worship leaders, it was Amos 5 that started it for me. The thought that God might not be interested in our songs, that our music and lifestyle might be out of sync, that we might just be making noise all this time — well, that thought got to me. I remember standing up on stage, kind of in a flow about all this, praying that God would give us his heart on all this, and the more I was praying that, the more I felt convinced that we didn't really want it.

The truth is that every time we talk about sponsoring a child, or getting out of our westernized comfort zone, everybody gets quiet, everybody gets powering down, tuning out. And I went on this rant, with a fresh zeal even though I felt like I really didn't have any wisdom on it at all.

We are blessed to be a blessing. We have talent in order to give it out, to distribute it to others. It doesn't matter if people get offended by our having a clearly religious agenda; what matters is that we take on our role of living by what God says.

I read this great scripture in Romans 15 in *The Message* version, and it said that "strength is for service, not status." I remember reading that, and reading it over and over again, and sharing it, and saying, "You know we've been empowered, we've been blessed, we live in a great country, we have more than we could ever possibly need – what is all this stuff for?"

Will we put our money where our mouths are? Will we put our hearts out there? And so, I think it is the role of the Church – not the role of government, not the role of just activists and rock stars, it is the responsibility of the Church to reach out to the poor and disenfranchised – that's why we have all this stuff, so that we can use it, not wallow in it.

I had a really good friend die. In fact, he killed himself and I remember being totally confused by the news. Instead of it having the effect of making me want to live life to the full, I just found myself feeling really overwhelmed by it all. This guy had it all, and yet he felt like nothing he could do would make a difference.

It's like the old idea of being a pebble on a beach: small and insignificant on our own . . . it's easy to think that we're not affecting anything, even to think that sending our money off to worthy causes doesn't really accomplish all that much after all. But what are we really doing with our lives? I think that question will always ring. And I believe in a lot of ways that I may not see what I want to see in my lifetime, but

I want to be found really passionately transferring that idea to my kids and hopefully they'll do the same with theirs. And as a part of my lineage and legacy, they'll carry it on, just like I am with the generations that have gone before me. Whether things are good or bad, we're going to choose to live a certain way: not trying to accumulate more and more wealth, but trying to bring about more and more change.

I had never really seen the connection between being a worshipper and being active in social justice, until recently. Society and industry tell us that we work hard and gain a certain level of status, and it's a lie that we all buy into. When we're young and full up with nothing more than aspirations and goals it all makes sense to live this way – to aim for a life where success is defined by wealth. And when those dreams start to come into reality there's a temptation to sit back and say, "Well, I deserve it." But the truth is different . . . any platform we gain, any influence we seem to have is there for a bigger reason.

QUESTION 2: COULD WE BE ABOUT TO WORK OUT THAT POVERTY IS NOT QUITE WHAT WE THOUGHT IT WAS?

The thing is, I know people with a lot of money, but they're poor. In fact, they're beyond poor – they're completely bankrupt. In spirit. You can probably see some of them for yourself too – the ones who are so cocooned in their own world that they don't see what else is happening around them: all that matters is what's going on in their own headspace; all that counts is them.

So there's a lot of poverty going on down on Wall Street. And there's poverty elsewhere too; suffering can be found everywhere and some of it is white-collar, and some of it is blue-collar and some of it is no-collar. We can't deny the physical kind – the sort that starves the body as well as the spirit. We'll come back to that, but this poverty that's resting on so many of us Westerners with healthy bank accounts needs to be addressed.

It's the kind that keeps us sheltered and blindfolded to all the other problems in this world. It's the kind that limits us, that makes us less than we could be, less than we can be.

It's the kind that might accept that giving has something to do with putting some cash in the collection bucket, but doesn't go much further than that.

It's the kind that doesn't even begin to understand that giving is a state of mind and a state of heart.

But there's something that is changing. People are beginning to wake up to the fact that stepping over people on the way into church is not OK. We're beginning to understand that a little bit of money given here and there is not what it's all about. We're beginning to understand that when it comes to how our lives affect those around us, God's raising the bar for each of us.

In the past many of us have signed up to the myth of thinking that we Westerners are the great hope of the world: we go, fix things up and sit back and wait for the gratitude and praise to flood in. We couldn't be more wrong.

I think I know this change is real because I've seen it in my own life. Gradually, over the past few years, I've begun to see that the problems of poverty are bigger than I first thought, that they demand more of me as I wake up to wanting to be a part of fixing them. It's a challenge, and one that I'm loving.

This challenge is teaching many of us that not only can poverty be found in the wealth of the West, but the ones we traditionally think of as being poor have more needs than just food and water.

To see child soldiers in Uganda, little children who have been told over and over how they will never have the option of being anything other than a killer ... it's as brutal a life as you can imagine. And it demands more than simple statements and half-smiles.

I've seen it in South Africa too. I spent six hours in an orphanage, sitting across from people full of talent and potential but with no hope beyond a daily meal and a safe place to sleep. Surely God made life to be about more than that? I've seen it in the face of a two-year-old girl who was chained to her bed and left for dead. How does any human being do that to a child? The people at the orphanage have changed her name to Nalede (meaning "star"), but how far does she have to travel before she finds herself living a life where all her potential can be realized?

It seems to me that the issue of poverty – whether it's spiritual or physical – is a symptom of identity. As a songwriter I've been trying to address this without being goofy or obvious about it, and I'm learning what happens if we can get people to sing eternal truths about themselves over and over – that they are not forgotten, that God knows each of us by name. And I believe that something happens when you sing that kind of thing, that gradually we can start to address some of the problems that poverty brings beside physical hunger and thirst.

In that way it's important that we work out what – and who – else worship is for: yes, worship propels us out, but it can – and should – also invite people in. It's a means of helping people believe that they were created with purpose, intention and design, they didn't just sneak into the earth unannounced.

So could we be capable of seeing poverty as something different? I think we can. I think we can see it all around us as well as seeing it in different forms. And best of all, I think we're slowly beginning to see it as something that we must not turn away from. Wherever we see it – from white-collar to dusty shanty town – poverty should be the catalyst for our action.

QUESTION 3: I'M JUST A PEBBLE AND THIS OCEAN IS SO VAST, HOW CAN I EVER HOPE TO MAKE A DIFFERENCE?

It's true, we have a problem here. We think that there's no way that our lives can make a difference, what with the problems being stacked so high and our influence being so little.

I've seen this clearly in South Africa. Apartheid may be over, but there remains a lot of residue throughout the country. I have a few good friends out there whose identity still has this big crack through it. They're good people, they love God and they love each other. But they are imprisoned in their own history, in their own world, and they really have been led to believe, generation upon generation, that this is as far as I can go, that this life is as good as it gets. But to look at them it's obvious that their potential is great, that what they could do with these insecurities and myths cut out could be truly remarkable. After all, the country is so rich in resources and beauty, who wouldn't believe that South Africa could have a more significant future ahead of it?

And then I think back to life at home, and I see the same things: lives with cracks in, hands tied by nothing more than a belief that they are held in place by chains and ropes, when the truth is that they're free all along. Our potential is great – greater than we might actually believe.

If ever I want proof of this, all I need to do is to think about the way in which, over the last few years, people's understanding of the links between worship and justice has grown. It's happened to me; I never really saw it before. I was fine with signing up for the importance of worship, I still had a heart for justice, but I never saw that they were hand in glove before. But lately it's all changed, leading me to see that they are absolutely synonymous, that worship goes far beyond music and sounds and songs; it's all about the intentions of the heart and the work of our hands.

For some of us there may be lightbulb moments or Damascus Road conversions that leave us suddenly convinced that we can make a difference. But for most of us it's not like that at all. Working out that we can make a difference is often a gradual process, a slow growth away from thinking that our potential is limited towards the bright realization that, with God, all things are possible. There are no limits to what we Christians can do when it comes to fighting poverty. We can be part of the solution, part of the fix.

And it starts with taking a look around and realizing that poverty and disease surround us, but understanding that seeing the world as it is does not negate us from doing something.

QUESTION 4: DO WE REALLY WANT TO CHANGE?

OK, so many of us see the world for the state it really is in, and many of us in the Church agree that something needs to be done, but how many of us are actually getting on and dealing with it? From where I sit I'm watching a very sluggish American Church allude to the fact that there are problems out there but not actually doing anything about it. Surely that can't be the way Jesus intended things to be?

I believe in a kingdom principle that says take care of what you've got because it's yours. I heard this story – more of a parable, really – about a builder who had a very rich man come to him and say, "Hey, I want you to build this house for me." He handed over the cash and left the builder to get on with the job. And the guy started to build it but he cut corners, he pocketed whatever money he thought he could get away with. On the surface things looked fine, but the reality was that this was a shabby house, poorly made and all messed up.

When the builder had finished he handed over the keys to the owner, but he just gave them straight back. "No," he said, "this house was for you."

I'm guessing that any of us in the builder's situation at that point would have wished that we'd done a better job.

Our selfish tendencies lead us to say that if it's for someone else we'll just tip our hat to it, see what we can do and make it look decent on the surface but not really try all that hard to fix it completely. And I think it's the same thing with the earth and with humanity: it's like we go, "Hey, it's not really benefiting me, it's not really costing me to go and serve others. I'll send a check every now and again, I'll do something that means I don't have to get my fingers dirty." All that time the Lord is reminding us that this world we're building requires a little more care to be taken of it.

Living in America means that we have to work a little harder to engage. There's not a lot of coverage in the American news about real stuff going on in Africa or other parts of the world scarred by poverty. It has to get to genocide levels before people start crying foul in America. And, amazingly for some of us Christians, the people who cry foul first are the ones who have probably a better cultural and world view: a lot of actors and entertainers from all over the place who travel and are more exposed to things. Some of us take this as a sign that poverty is best left to the liberals, or that engaging in these issues is not something for ordinary families with bills and payments to keep on top of. But it's just not true: there's real stuff going on and we all have to do something about it.

I love the fact that we've advanced technologically – that we now have a good chance of being better informed thanks to the internet –

but I am concerned that in the name of our advances we've become more closed off than opened up. We've become more tunnel-visioned, focused on myspace, my world, my news, my internet and my computer, as opposed to allowing ourselves to have a better view of what life is like for others.

Growing up in church my whole life, like many others I've been watching how this subject immediately polarizes people. Mention poverty to some and they'll reply by saying something like, "You know, I'm glad you have that compassion for those who are struggling, but I have bills and I've got to go to work tomorrow morning." People can tune out so easily: it blows my mind how we've been adopted but we shun the idea of adopting others. We just sort of cut that off, or tune it out, and it's something that is quite amazing to me.

But it doesn't have to be this way. I started realizing as a songwriter that I might be able to awaken and mobilize and catalyze some things in my little world, but the songs are only ever going to be a soundtrack at best; what each of us can be is the clearest and most potent living example of a life lived in step with God. We can put into action the possibilities that are found in a life that allows God to set the course.

Change doesn't have to be an impossibility. It can be real, normal and incredibly exciting.

QUESTION 5: CAN WE FACE UP TO THE PROBLEMS THAT NEED OUR ATTENTION?

I think we could have a bit of heaven on earth. I think we could be operating on what we were called to do all along. I think that the potential for what the Church can do could go through the roof.

But there are some things that are holding us back, and we really need to deal with them properly.

LOVE IN ACTION

There are so many things in the Bible about love and loving one another. The only way people are going to know we're Christians is by us loving one another, not by the coolness of our architecture or the sonic quality of our music. Surely it all has to come down to love and the way we treat each other – those inside the Church with us as well as those outside its walls.

I heard a statistic that made me think: if every American who considered him or herself a Christian just tithed their income to their local church then poverty worldwide could be eradicated and dealt with. There might even be a few billion dollars left over. It staggers me to think about the fact that one in three people in the world are Christians, yet almost as many try to live on less than $2 a day.

Can we deal with this? Can we get our heads around the fact that we hold so much potential in our hands? Can we get over ourselves and put love into action in a way that radically changes things all over the planet?

UNITY

When Martin Luther nailed his complaints about the Catholic Church to the door, the pope of the time had something interesting to say. He told Luther that he believed they could work things out, but if Luther carried on pressing for change then the Church would never stop splitting. That's one of the most amazing prophetic statements ever made.

Now, Luther's actions are seen by us Protestants as a defining moment, but at the same time the Church has been splitting ever since. These layers of theological difference that run across the world have left us with wars fought over schisms, over tiny differences of opinion. I hear friends of mine saying all the time that the Church is the hope of the world, and I believe it 100 percent, but I don't believe that the Church in its current state is the hope of the world. We need to be unified. Full stop. We have to say as a Church worldwide what we agree on, and at least agree that there's a dying world out there that needs our focus and attention – and the only way we're going to be able to do that is to come together. We don't have to agree on our theologies or doctrines, but we do have to agree on some things. We have to agree to work together to put Christ's love into action.

UNDERSTANDING

Finally, we have to fix this one: we have to open our eyes. As individuals throughout the Church we have to truly see the need.

I have a great friend from Zimbabwe who comes over and preaches in the States from time to time. I've been there when he's been addressing crowds of thousands, primarily African American people. He's asked how many of them want to go to Africa some day. Perhaps 90 percent of the hands in the building go up. He tells them to keep their hands held high and he asks them another question: "How many of you have a passport?" Eighty percent of those hands go down.

The uncomfortable truth is that we do a lot of talking but we don't really prepare to put it into action. Even something as simple as having a passport ready for when that moment comes. It's not enough of a priority, not enough of a passion to say, "I'm ready to go." It's been alarming and saddening to see it happen. People need to see the problem – but blaming the TV producers for not telling us enough won't work as an excuse.

EPILOGUE

Bishop Graham Cray

WORSHIP-SONG WRITERS ARE AMONG THE MOST INFLUENTIAL TEACHING THEOLOGIANS OF THEIR GENERATION. MOST OF THE TALKS AND SERMONS I GIVE AND THE ARTICLES I WRITE ARE FORGOTTEN, COMPARATIVELY QUICKLY. BUT FREQUENTLY REPEATED WORSHIP SONGS EMBED THEMSELVES IN THE MEMORY. THEY ARE MEANT TO. GOD MADE MUSIC TO WORK LIKE THAT. THAT'S WHY WE ARE TO "SING PSALMS AND HYMNS AND SPIRITUAL SONGS TO ONE ANOTHER, MAKING MELODY TO THE LORD IN OUR HEARTS" (EPHESIANS 5:19, NRSV). MUSIC IN WORSHIP IS "TO THE LORD," FOR GOD ABOVE ALL, BUT IT IS ALSO "TO ONE ANOTHER," AN ACT OF MUTUAL ENCOURAGEMENT IN LOVING AND SERVING GOD. IT IS THIS THAT MAKES IT SUCH A POWERFUL TEACHING MEDIUM AS WELL.

What we sing, or never sing, profoundly influences our spiritual growth and understanding. Because we may not know a lot more than the theology we sing, our sung repertoire needs to reflect the whole counsel and the full heart of God. If that is so, our songwriters need to be on a journey of deepening spiritual vision and understanding. CompassionArt is the result of such a journey.

The Bible is crucial to that journey. It lies at the heart of all trustworthy Christian learning. Christ is the only Lord and Savior, but to know Christ, and to see life from Christ's perspective, we need the Bible, and to allow God to keep teaching us from the Bible. There is a famous saying that "the Lord has more light and truth yet to break forth out of his holy Word." Originating from Pastor John Robinson's address to the Pilgrim Fathers in 1620, it was the inspiration for a hymn, which first appeared in 1835, "The Lord Hath Yet More Light and Truth to Break Forth from His Word." Sometimes we get that light and truth simply by reading the Bible and praying. Many excellent songs have been written as a consequence of studying and meditating on scripture. But the more radical lessons seem to be learned by another route. We seem to wear sets of blinkers when we read the Bible. Some are cultural, some more connected to our personal histories, but they tend to filter those aspects that are either beyond our imagination or "too challenging." Strange though it may seem, to learn from the Word we need to learn more about the world. It is as we learn more about real life for other people, other cultures and the world beyond our own normal experience that we are faced with new questions and challenges. As believers we can then go to the Bible to find answers to questions we have never faced before.

All the CompassionArt songwriters travel internationally. Culturally they are all raised in the West (sorry, Darlene!) but they have all traveled south and east. Any Christian from an affluent culture who travels to the developing world finds him or herself facing new questions, about poverty and justice, about HIV and life expectancy, about the contrast between cultures that throw away food and cultures where people die for lack of it. Some of the chapters in this book tell those stories. Whether it was Matt, Martin, Stu or Graham in India, Michael, Chris, Darlene or Israel in Africa, Steven or Andy in China or even me (definitely not a songwriter!) in Madagascar, you find yourself asking how you sing the Lord's song after what you have just seen. As a believer you go back to the Bible with these questions, and only then do you start to see God's heart for the poor, for children and for justice, in passages where you hadn't noticed them before. Light and truth break forth from his Word. It was always there but we needed some new questions before we could see it. Once we have seen it we have to act on its truth and walk in its light. This or some parallel journey prepared eleven other songwriters for Martin and Anna's invitation to join them in Scotland to write songs together for the poor.

Some of the songs written that week directly refer to God's heart for the poor and will for justice, and call us to follow. Others are songs of proclamation and praise. But they come from a renewed scriptural vision of a God who, in Jesus, addresses all the needs of his fallen, rebellious and needy creation. That is why we "Shout Praise" and call him "King of Wonders."

While we were together in Scotland we began each day with scripture, determined to understand the scale of God's purposes and the depth of his heart.

THE SCALE OF DIVINE COMMITMENT

We sometimes miss the sheer scale of God's commitment to the world because we start too late in the biblical story. The story does not begin with the Fall and end with forgiveness, it travels from creation to new creation, creation restored. Salvation is personal. We each need the forgiveness won on the cross, but salvation is more than personal: it is for the whole creation, and forgiveness restores us to our part in God's plan to make everything new.

The doctrine of creation tells us that the created order is good; God said so when he made it, and when he made his human stewards, in his own image, he said that it was very good. This world and its human stewards are God's masterpieces. That is why sin and sickness, poverty and injustice are such an offense to God. They mar his masterpiece and fail to treat his works of art with the value he gives them.

As a consequence of the Fall we are all marred masterpieces. Sin severely mars the Creator's work, but can never erase it. Divine artistry still shows through every human life. And divine love never withdraws. God does not give up on his fallen stewards or his broken creation, despite the most extreme provocation from his rebellious people. This is seen in both the Old and the New Testaments.

God's love for his people is movingly expressed through Hosea. Hosea 11 tells of God's feelings for his chosen people, feelings that parents have for their children, feelings of love and devotion. Yet his affection was not mirrored. The more he called them, the more God's people wandered away. Like any parent, God had taught them to walk . . .

> I took them up in my arms;
> but they did not know that I healed them.
> I led them with cords of human kindness,
> with bands of love;
> I was to them like those
> who lift infants to their cheeks.
> I bent down to them and fed them.
>
> Hosea 11:3-4, NRSV

God contemplates their future – a time marked by more wanderings and rejections, an increase of violence and a decrease in justice. It is as if they are determined to turn their backs on their Maker. Yet he cannot give them the punishment they deserve:

> How can I give you up, Ephraim?
> How can I hand you over, O Israel? . . .
> My heart recoils within me;
> my compassion grows warm and tender.
> I will not execute my fierce anger;
> I will not again destroy Ephraim;
> for I am God and no mortal, –
> the Holy One in your midst,
> and I will not come in wrath.
>
> Hosea 11:8–9, NRSV

This is what the heart of God says: "How can I give you up?"

In the New Testament God shows his unfailing love for fallen flesh and blood human beings by going even further than before and becoming a flesh and blood human being. As John 1:14 explains, "The Word became flesh and lived among us." The incarnation, God's Son becoming human, was not only an unavoidable stepping stone to the atonement. He did not become human temporarily, just so that he could die in our place. It was an act of permanent identification with his creation and an extraordinary expression of God's pleasure (Colossians 1:19).

When Jesus rose from the dead, his renewed body, which cannot die and which is his for all eternity, was also the promise and prototype of the renewed body the Father has prepared for everyone who believes in him. That is what Paul means when he says that "Christ has been raised from the dead, the firstfruits of those who have died" (1 Corinthians 15:20, NRSV).

Jesus' ascension is not about getting him offstage, so that the Holy Spirit can come. It is about his bodily entry into the Father's presence, to intercede for us. Paul says in Colossians 2:9 that "in him the whole fullness of deity dwells bodily" (note the present tense!).

When Christ returns there will be a final judgment, but this will also be the time when the whole of creation is renewed.

It is in the final pages of scripture that we get a clearer idea of what this might look like. Revelation describes a scene where:

> the home of God is among mortals.
> He will dwell with them;
> they will be his peoples,
> and God himself will be with them;
> he will wipe every tear from their eyes.
> Death will be no more;
> mourning and crying and pain will be no more,
> for the first things have passed away . . .
> See, I am making all things new.
>
> Revelation 21:3–5, NRSV

Our future hope is not to leave the earth and go to heaven, it is to be a part of the redeemed human race in an earth and heaven made new.

God will never be divorced from the physical creation: he will renew it. As Tom Wright says,

> God, after all, is the creator; he has no interest in leaving earth to rot and making do for all eternity with only one half of the original creation. God intends to flood the whole cosmos, heaven and earth together, with his presence and grace, and when that happens the new world that

results, in which Jesus himself will be the central figure, is to be the inheritance for which Jesus' people are longing.*

Or, as another writer put it. "God wills that we cannot know heaven without also knowing earth."†

Why all this theology? The implications are profound. What God has done in Jesus shows us that our God is committed to flesh and blood. Flesh and blood, redeemed and freed from death and decay, has an eternal future. The ordinary things we do with flesh and blood are holy, including making music. Music in worship involves flesh and blood singing back to the Creator of flesh and blood, who himself became flesh and blood. And, in the service which he gave us, at the heart of worship, we hear him saying, "This is my body, this is my blood, given for you."

DIVINE DISSATISFACTION

But worship is inseparable from justice and mercy.

> Take away from me the noise of your songs;
> I will not listen to the melody of your harps.
> But let justice roll down like waters,
> and righteousness like an ever-flowing stream.
> Amos 5:23–24, NRSV

For when flesh and blood starves, God is grieved. When flesh and blood suffers, God is grieved. When flesh and blood is oppressed, God

* Tom Wright, *Paul for Everyone: The Prison Letters: Ephesians, Philippians* (Westminster John Knox Press, 2004).
† David Runcorn, *Choice, Desire and the Will of God* (SPCK, 2003).

is grieved. When the flesh and blood stewards of the earth abuse his creation, God is grieved.

His redeemed people are to share his commitment. That is why they have been redeemed. The things that grieve him should grieve us. There is such a thing as godly dissatisfaction. Some of our songs should express his dissatisfaction.

But be warned. God's dissatisfaction is also his call to action.

It is sobering to compare the book of Psalms, which was the hymn book of the rebuilt temple after Israel's return from exile, with our hymn and song books. There are three primary types of psalm: songs of praise and worship, rejoicing in who God is and what he has done to redeem; songs of lament and prayer, from situations where God does not yet seem to be acting like a redeemer; and songs of thanksgiving or testimony in response to what God has done answering his people's prayer. Our song books have the first and the third, but where is the lament? We are good at expressing intimacy and high praise, but what about outrage and agony? A passionate and compassionate God seeks a passionate and compassionate people who share his mind and heart.

In the Old Testament we read how God hates "the lover of violence" (Psalm 11:5, NRSV). Proverbs 6 adds to this list of things that the Lord hates, coming up with seven traits that are an "abomination" to God:

> haughty eyes, a lying tongue,
> and hands that shed innocent blood,
> a heart that devises wicked plans,
> feet that hurry to run to evil,
> a lying witness who testifies falsely,
> and one who sows discord in a family.
>
> Proverbs 6:17–19, NRSV

The theme continues in Isaiah 59, where God is "displeased" by the lack of justice in society and "appalled" that nobody steps up to intervene on behalf of the defenseless.

Yet God does not walk away from our failings. In Hosea God's outrage and agony combine: "How can I give you up?" he asks.

That agony and outrage takes shape when God's Son becomes flesh and blood: Jesus, who when he saw the crowds, had compassion for them (Matthew 9:36) as well as looking at them "with anger; he was grieved at their hardness of heart and said to the man, 'Stretch out your hand.' He stretched it out, and his hand was restored" (Mark 3:5, NRSV).

Nowhere is that seen more clearly than in Gethsemane. We read how Jesus "began to be distressed and agitated" explaining to his disciples that he is "deeply grieved, even to death" and that they should stay there and not drift off. Throwing himself to the ground he prays that – if it is at all possible – his Father in heaven might change the course of what is it come. But he follows his words with these: "yet, not what I want, but what you want" (Mark 14:34, 36, NRSV).

By the Spirit we also call God "Abba"; it is the great word that expresses intimacy with the Father. But Abba is also a Gethsemane word. Jesus went through the agonies of the cross to redeem a people who would agonize with him over his lost creatures and broken world.

We are adopted into God's family to play a part in the family business – a business that works for "the healing and rebirth of the entire created order" (Romans 8:18–27).

It was never intended that we should share in the Son's fellowship with the Father if we don't also share in the Son's mission from the Father. We become the bridge people, joining a broken and lost world to the broken heart of God.

CompassionArt is not primarily about songs. It is about honoring a God of extraordinary passion and commitment. It is about worship with lives as well as lips. It is about the poor being as much on the Church's heart as they are on God's heart. It is about a church that no longer believes that the point of Christianity is being saved, because it knows that the point of being saved is to work with God until earth and heaven are made new. It is about a world-transforming faith rather than a world-withdrawing faith. It is also about a world and a church where worship and service, justice and beauty, compassion and art belong together.

+Graham Cray
April 2008

THE STORY OF COMPASSIONART

HOW DID IT START?

CompassionArt is a new international charity founded by Delirious? frontman Martin Smith and his wife, Anna.

WHO IS COMPASSIONART?

We are a global community, an underground adventure, a map being drawn as we speak that connects wealth with poverty, art with hope, compassion with despair. We are starting with twelve of the best-known Christian recording artists, who have come together to create an album and a book, with all proceeds and royalties going to break the hold of poverty on people's lives around the world. But we're not stopping there; CompassionArt is evolving to connect, inspire and release compassion all over the world.

WHAT'S THE FIRST STEP?

January 2008: twelve Christian artists gathered in Scotland to write – and later record – a new set of songs to inspire and equip the church. A year later and those songs have evolved into an album and a book.

WHO GETS THE HELP?

All the money raised is divided two ways; half gets split between the four headline CompassionArt-supported projects. The other half is divided among twelve charities nominated by each of the twelve CompassionArt songwriters.

COMPASSIONART HEADLINE PROJECTS

India and Cambodia : *Hand of Hope*
Offers relief and restoration for families caught up in Mumbai's sex trade, and food and education for children trying to survive on a rubbish dump in Phnom Penh.
www.joycemeyer.org/OurMinistries/HandofHope

Brazil : *Ray of Hope*
Every week in remote parts of Brazil, the Ray of Hope team takes to the river to meet the needs of children: food, education, support, advice, clothing and medical aid. Their compassion heads deep into the jungle.
www.rayofhopeamazon.com

Uganda : *Watoto*
From orphaned children to abused mothers, Watoto restores hope to people whose lives have been devastated by suffering. By providing creative life centers, Watoto encourages artistic education and plans for a better future for all.
www.watoto.com

Global: *Stop The Traffik*
Stop The Traffik is a global movement that works against the trafficking of people. It has more than 1,000 member organizations in fifty countries and a grassroots following of ordinary activists around the world.
www.stopthetraffik.org

COMPASSIONART NOMINATED CHARITIES

Living Hope Community Centre — *Michael W. Smith*
Plays a vital role in the prevention, care, treatment and support of people infected and affected by HIV and AIDS, and other chronic illnesses in Cape Town, South Africa.
www.livinghope.co.za

Links International — *Martin & Anna Smith*
From micro-enterprise to clean water, Links International has been serving and inspiring the church to have an impact on local communities around the world since 1985.
www.linksinternational.org.uk

Hope Rwanda — *Darlene Zschech*
Provides sustainable solutions to poverty that lead to the restoration of hope for the people of Rwanda, primarily by building homes for widows and orphans.
www.hoperwanda.org

Baby Watoto — *Chris Tomlin*
In Uganda, abandoned children — from newborns to two-year-olds — are given care, medical support, a loving environment and a future in a family as part of the Watoto Community.
www.watoto.com

Compassion UK – *Matt Redman*
Compassion seeks out some of the world's most vulnerable children
and through individual sponsors provides them with the means to
break the cycle of poverty and create a viable future.
www.compassionuk.org

Caring For Ex-Offenders and The Regeneration Trust – *Tim Hughes*
Working across prisons and estates in London, CFEO seeks to enable
prisoners to break the cycle of crime and reintegrate successfully
back into society. The Trust works in deprived housing estates in
London to help children and single-parent families who suffer from
the effects of poverty, and to prevent others from falling into
poverty.
www.caringforexoffenders.org

Shaohannah's Hope – *Steven Curtis Chapman*
Dedicated to helping prospective adoptive parents overcome the
financial barriers associated with adoption. The charity awards
financial grants to qualified families already in the process of
adopting, depending on their need.
www.shaohannahshope.org

For The Silent – *Paul Baloche*
Working to bring an end to the sexual exploitation, trafficking and
slavery of children worldwide.
forthesilent.org

St. Stephens – *Andy Park*

For over forty years St. Stephens has worked among those addicted to drugs in Hong Kong. Founded by Jackie Pullinger, the charity has led thousands of people to faith and new hope.
www.ststephenssociety.com

Restoring the Sound – *Graham Kendrick*

Preventing African schoolgoers from getting caught in a culture of gangs and violence. Restoring the Sound uses music as a means to help people better themselves and their community.
www.restoringthesound.com

Beanz Meanz Livez – *Stu Garrard*

In the UK alone 88% of Britons have an estimated £10 in small change somewhere lost in their house. BML provides a means of collecting these coins and uses the money to provide clean water for families and children in India.
www.beanzmeanzlivez.com

Lakewood Missions – *Israel Houghton*

Reaches out with hope and compassion through medical and humanitarian efforts, to assist people in great need.
www.lakewoodmissions.org (website currently under construction)